When Are Your PARENTS Coming to Get You?

Wait...What? These are MY kids!
I am their mother!

By ROXANA HACKETT

Ark House Press
PO Box 1722, Port Orchard, WA 98366 USA
PO Box 1321, Mona Vale NSW 1660 Australia
PO Box 318 334, West Harbour, Auckland 0661 New Zealand
arkhousepress.com

Cataloguing in Publication Data:
Title: When Are Your Parents Coming to Get You?
ISBN: 9780994596833 (pbk.)
Subjects: Parenting, Christian Living,
Other Authors/Contributors: Hackett, Roxana

Edited by Amanda Sauer
Cover by Brad Smith Design
Layout by initiateagency.com

Endorsements

"If you are a mom trying to raise godly children in the twenty-first century and have ever felt at a loss navigating our toxic Western culture, then this book is for you. Roxana Hackett's disarming and personal style is less of a how-to manual, and something more like the diary of a companion on the journey—a mother who has been there, and still is. Honest, witty, at times raw, and always engaging, she weaves her own experiences and observations into more than just nuggets of poignant wisdom. She makes you aware that you are not alone and that it's okay not to have all the answers. This is a worthy and life-giving read!"

Bernie Herms, Composer and producer / and **Natalie Grant**, Singer and songwriter

---

"Roxana writes with transparency and humor, bringing color and a few awkward cringes to each page. Oh the joys of parenting! Can hardly wait to finish the book!"

Lori E. Dixon, Author of *Soles Defining Souls* (LKM Publishing, 2015); mother of two

---

"There are countless books out there offering advice or instructions for parents. But, at the end of the day, what most mothers need is for another mother to simply say, 'Me, too!' In her new book, *When Are Your Parents Coming to Get You?* Roxana pulls back the curtain on motherhood and does just that. Her transparency is refreshing and her humor is contagious. Each chapter will have you nodding in complete agreement and believing that, perhaps, you're doing okay at this parenting gig after all."

Stacy Edwards, Author of *Devotions from the Front Porch* (Thomas Nelson, 2016), *Devotions for Christmas* (Zondervan, 2016), *Devotions for Easter* (Zondervan 2017) *and Devotions from the Kitchen Table* (Thomas Nelson, 2017); speaker; mother of five StacyJEdwards.com

---

"In her book *When Are Your Parents Coming to Get You?* Roxana takes readers along her own parenting journey and offers biblical wisdom for the real-life challenges parents face. Roxana's vulnerable approach to sharing the everyday challenges makes this book easy to relate to and relevant for today's parents. For parents seeking wisdom for raising their children, this book is a great resource."

Michelle Coomer, Author of *foreseen. forgiven. FREE.* (WESTBOW press, 2015); mother of four

---

"I feel like Roxana has been a fly on the wall in my house! Her honesty and humor are so refreshing. She delivers encouragement for all of us moms in the trenches!"

Cari Jimmy Garrett, Mother of three

"I LOVE this book! Roxana is a gifted writer! All her stories are either hilarious, relatable, or gut-wrenching. I am so glad to have this book to lean on when going through my own parenting."

Barby Harmon, Mother of two

"I love Roxana's down-to-earth writing style and true-to-life examples from her own family. Her sense of humor shines through, and her raw honesty is a refreshing break from our whitewashed 'social media polished' lives that we read about and compare ourselves to on Facebook. As a mom of four, I love her storytelling and find pieces of my own family in each chapter. Her use of Scripture is inspiring and challenging all at once. What a great read to lift me up, make me laugh, and inspire me to be a better mom!"

Katrina Henderson, Mother of four

"Roxana writes beautifully! She is able to validate (often humorously) our daily parenting struggles."

Nancy Wanjohi Juma, Mother of four

To my mom, Dimitrita
To my grandparents, Virginia and Gheorghe
To my husband, Donny
And my kids, Harrison and Sofia
I love you with all my heart.

Nothing beats the wit and wisdom of another mom.
—Marisa Cohen, *Red Book Magazine*

Contents

Introduction

Why am I writing this book?
I am writing this book because I am in the parenting trenches trying to survive this very rewarding but very tough job. No one really prepares you for being a parent (a good one anyway). In any case, we felt unprepared. My husband and I got married in 1997 and waited seven years to have children.

We wanted to enjoy our new life as a newlywed couple, travel to exotic places, pursue artistic careers, become rich and famous (ha-ha), enjoy silent mornings, sleep in late, have movie marathons, and fly off to Rome on a moment's notice, as writer Nora Ephron puts it. We did do some of these things, but flying off to Rome did not happen, neither did visiting exotic places, except to go to my home country of Romania, and had one stop over in Cronenberg, Germany, for ONE day! (That was amazing!)

Eventually after pursuing different volatile careers (because we were young and immature and thought we knew what was good for us better than God), and after the practical outweighed the abandon (as it usually does), we realized we were getting older. I was twenty-nine and my husband thirty-nine, and so we were ready to start a family. At first (after about one hundred pregnancy tests, and lots of tears), God blessed us with a son—and after four more years, He blessed us with a daughter. We would have liked more children, but it turned out I had difficulty getting pregnant in the first place with both the kids, and since we had one of each we were very grateful.

So, you may ask, "What's up with the title of this book . . . *When Are Your Parents Coming to Get You? . . .* It's kind of weird." Yes, it does sound like we don't want our children and we can't wait to get rid of them! I assure you it is quite the opposite. These two precious children are solely our own, but ever since our son was little, my husband would tease him by asking him:

"When are your parents coming to get you?"

"But YOU are my parents!"

"Really? For how long?"

"Forever!!!"

"Oh no! Not forever!!" and they would laugh and giggle together.

My husband says this to tease our kids, of course, but it comes from a place of awe and sudden realization that these two beautiful creatures are ours to keep and we are fully responsible to do a good job raising them. Also, this saying has a nuance of epiphany in it; these children weren't here before, but now here they both are standing flesh-and-blood in front of us looking to us for complete guidance, depending on us in every way.

We love our kids like crazy people (as you love yours), and we think to ourselves, *Dear God, we hope we are not going to fail at this parenting thing . . .* Personally, I have plenty of days when I feel discouraged, and filled with a sense of unworthiness, sure that other parents are much more efficient at rearing their children than I am. (And some of my friends have six kids, not two!) Well, in any case, this is how the title of the book was born.

What should you expect when reading this book?

As you can see on the cover, there is no "PhD" at the end of my name, nor any other scholastic titles. Aside from going to college for three years studying child psychology, I do not possess any accolades regarding child rearing. The only merit I have is being a full-time parent—and if you are reading this book, we share the same merit and that is what this book is about. We are confederates in parenting, and in this book through many practical and personal examples, I am reaching out to you, inviting you to partake in this journey of raising our children. Through a very transparent tone, I will try to ignite an emotional contact between us as parents, and perhaps you will sympathize, empathize, and recognize yourselves in all the different circumstances and predicaments. Hopefully you won't think I am completely insane, and that you will reciprocate my emotions, frustrations, and triumphs. This book is conversational, at times humorous, tackling to express my current parenting encounters.

Our daughter is in elementary school, while our son entered middle school. They are very different from each other in many ways, including personalities, with one of them providing most of the material for this book! (You'll have to figure out which one is the challenging one.) I don't want to give the impression that I prefer or love one child over the other, but the fact is that one of them has always made my parenting more stimulating! (I hear that's the case in other households as well.)

This is a Christian parenting book, so in all of my chapters I will substantiate my illustrations and opinions with Bible verses. I feel God is calling me to write this book right now, rather than later—and why not, since I am smack in the heat of it. This book serves as a therapeutic and visceral purpose for me, but also as an engagement between all of us parents to join each other in this wonderful, crazy, and perhaps the biggest excursion of our lives.

Psalm 127:3 says, "Children are a gift from the LORD; they are a reward from him." I believe parenting is a privilege (Latin word *privus* means "one's own"), an honor, and God trusts us with the responsibility of doing a good job at it. A lot is expected of us. We are here to take care of them physically, emotionally, spiritually—to cultivate, educate, construct, foster, nurture, train, elevate, and love them into becoming fully devoted followers of Christ, as my pastor says. Godly children turn into godly parents for future generations to come. Proverbs 22:6 instructs us to "Train up a child in the way that he should go; even when he is old he will not depart from it" (NKJV).

So, please come and let us join each other and share the ups and downs of parenting, because all we do every day is out of utter love. I am imparting on you a few words of a regular mom named Amanda who's also a friend of mine, just so you understand the tone of this book:

"Tucked the kids in. They then all had to promptly get out of bed to tell me the following:

'My eye hurts.'

'My head hurts. It will hurt while I'm asleep too.'

'I need to poop.'

'The poop won't come out.'

'I think I forgot to tell you something but I don't know what it is.'

'I think our elf lost her magic.'

'I need another drink.'

'What are you doing out there?'

'I still need to poop.'

For the love of everything, go to sleep. NOW."

Chapter 1

"It Should Only Last about Forty-Five Minutes"

Remember, that children who come into the world with their boxing gloves on, so to speak, are often the ones who become the biggest world changers.

—L. R. Knost

When our boy was born, we were beside ourselves! He was the first of his gender in my Romanian family since 1936, so you can imagine the excitement that stormed our hearts. He was much celebrated and long waited for. Unfortunately, no one on my side of the family got to see him except my mother who came to help me for the first three months after he was born.

This was my first pregnancy, so the neurotic planner that I am really wanted to have every single aspect of my being a new mother completely covered. I anticipated every scenario possible and had already implemented solutions for them. I made lists, charts, regimented feeding schedules, read all books pertaining to bringing up a baby, was extremely nervous, but confident in my preliminary plans, and ready to have this precious gem on February 23 . . . Well, God and our child had different plans.

A month prior to my due date, we were in church when I felt intense pressure and started having contractions. I was moving my body to and fro and shaking the pew with impatient pain. I signaled my husband that we had to leave. Quickly, we drove to the hospital (which was very close, thank God!), only to be told that our baby was ready to be born. Whaaat??!! My reveries of my water breaking in the middle of an upper class restaurant quickly dispersed . . . I had specific visions of that happening like in a dramatic movie scene, me getting up and exclaiming, "My water broke!" and then a flurry of concerned, yet excited people trying to escort us out of the restaurant, and bystanders gasping in nervous joy, "Aww, she's having a baby . . . how amazing."

ANYWAY. That scenario did not happen. The labor was short, and due to urgency and lack of time, I ended up giving birth in a black turtleneck.

Upon making sure the baby was healthy, the nurse said to me, "This baby has a will of its own!" *That's a good thing,* I am thinking to myself. Little did I know at the time that her words prefigured our son's extreme strong will, and fully encapsulated his very determined personality. My charts and feeding schedules completely useless now, I finally understood my friend's (already a seasoned mother) shocked look at seeing my rigid planning, and trying to suppress a smile by pressing her lips together in disapproval. I resented her discredit (I had mad hormones), thinking that I could not help being more organized and prepared than she was, but turned out that she was right. Our baby had colic, ate sporadically, cried most of the time, and the doctor said the colic should last three to four months. He did warn us that some kids remain colicky up to two years, but that is very rare.

Hooray! We qualified for that rare percentile and our boy was colicky up to nineteen months of age! Why? We don't know, except that every night around 1:30 a.m. he would cry for no apparent reason. We literally had to drive around the block many times to calm and lull him to sleep. During the day he was happy and playful, but at night we anticipated that awful hour.

It felt as though we were the exception to every "normal" rule of every parenting book I've read, for he also did not want to sleep in his own bed and protested severely. So, of course, after a long time taking turns sleeping with him for half our nights and then allowing him in our bed, we decided that it was about time that our three-year-old learned to stay in his own bed. Different parents and our pediatrician advised us to let him cry it out. They assured us that it should only last about forty-five minutes, after which he would be exhausted and finally give up all crying revolts and surrender into sleep. Simple enough, right?

NOPE.

Thirty minutes turned into forty-five, then into one hour, then into two hours of incessant, undeterred tears. We were in disbelief. He cried for six hours with quiet increments lasting for twenty minutes. I slept outside his door all night, overwhelmed with my own tears, compassion, frustration, confusion, and without a valid solution. I loved my kid and did not know how to handle his God-given bent. The Amplified Bible says "Train up a child in the way that he should go [and in keeping with his individual gift or bent]" (Proverbs 22:6). God made our child extremely focused, perseverant, resilient, and diligent. God said to Jeremiah: "Before I formed you in the womb I knew you, and before you were born I consecrated you" (Jeremiah 1:5 ESV).

Dr. James Dobson says that "unborn children are unique individuals with whom God is already acquainted."[1] The aforementioned verse in Jeremiah consoled me as I looked up the word "consecrated" in the *Oxford College Dictionary*. To consecrate means to "dedicate formally to a religious or divine purpose." So, then each one of our children is carefully selected by God and meticulously endowed with a precise individual mold, and uniquely configured with specific emotional and intellectual dimensions. Yes, this may be a formal understanding of my children (and of ourselves), but it gives me comfort and peace to know that God loves us so much and cares immensely about who He determines us to be. We as parents, then, are here to discern, understand, cultivate, harbor, and pray our way through parenting our treasured children. Psalm 139:13–16 beautifully assures us of all of this:

> You made all the delicate, inner parts of my body, and knit me together in my mother's womb. Thank you for making me wonderfully complex! . . . You watched me as I was being formed in utter seclusion, as I was woven together in the dark of the womb. You saw me before I was born. Every day of my life was recorded in your book.

These amazing verses resonated with me even deeper when I saw our daughter forming in my belly at twenty weeks. I remember thinking about people who have a hard time believing in God. All they need to see is a baby through an ultrasound. It moved me to tears when I spotted her tiny spine perfectly crafted, her heart beating with precision, all her delicate organs forming with innate dexterity. She was sucking her toes, swaying comfortably in a God-made womb—safe, content, and peacefully enjoying her existence. I am still filled with reverent wonder when I try to comprehend how our children came to be. They start so very little, smaller than a penny, and yet they have a heart, little cells eager to connect, generate, and flourish, masterful yet fragile veins and arteries forming in accurate harmony, and bones and muscles designed with intended artistry. I did nothing but have the honor of providing a space for God to skillfully design and flawlessly custom make our babies for us. Without a doubt, "Children are a gift from the Lord" (Psalm 127:3).

Our daughter was an easier baby, but she is now eight years old and there are a multitude of issues arising from peer pressure, the importance of outside beauty, being popular, fighting with her brother, having certain trendy dolls, and then trying to tame entitled attitudes.

Our two children are very different in so many ways, and they both provide lots of material for this book. In the following chapters, I will explore and illustrate many circumstances that pertain to their individual God-given bent.

Some children *may* stop after forty-five minutes of crying, and some may surprise and bewilder us into bracing ourselves for the most demanding, continually challenging, but also most exciting jobs created by God.

Chapter 2

Stop Yelling!

I have faults enough, but they are not, I hope,
of understanding. My temper I dare not vouch for.
—Jane Austen, *Pride and Prejudice*

I am not entirely sure what propels siblings to bicker and fight almost every minute they are together, but I have become convinced that it is pure entertainment for them. My daughter can play peacefully for hours, but when her brother enters the room, antennas go up instinctively detecting conflict time. And so the mutual agitation begins. My children are very talented at the art of squabble. They can pretty much spar each other over the most insignificant and petty things. Any daily confrontation will go on like this:

"Move over so I can sit on the couch!"

"No! You sit there. I was here first."

"Mommm! She's not moving over!"

"Well, then sit on the other side of the couch, son. It's a big couch. Not a big deal" (parenting from the kitchen while cooking).

So, out of spite, he sits right next to her, plopping his twelve-year-old body as hard as possible disrupting his sister's space. She then lashes out by elbowing him hard.

"Mom! She punched me!"

"No I didn't. I elbowed you."

"Same thing."

"No it isn't."

"Yes it is."

"No it isn't!! Shut your mouth!"

"Do not say 'shut your mouth.' Unacceptable!" (Still trying to parent as I peek around the corner with a warning finger at both of them.)

A more aggressive fight begins with both of them yelling at each other—stubborn as goats not budging—still defending their right to occupy that small space on a BIG couch! I cannot believe this! Really? It was never about sitting on the couch in the first place for my son. It was about having the power to win over his sister!

I am still trying to finish dinner, my husband is on his way home, sink is full of dirty dishes, my food is boiling and so is my blood. As their screaming continues, I step in, by now physically trying to separate them, and in my feeble attempt I end up yelling from the top of my lungs: "STOP YELLING!"

They both look at me very confused and say, "But you just yelled at us, Mom." Yeah, well it's different. They made me yell. They brought it out of me . . . I am very frustrated with the whole (stupid) thing and I send them to their rooms. I yelled and feel badly. I should be more patient. Another parent would have had control and wisdom to calmly deal with the situation and find a perfect solution. I am the worst parent on the planet. I feel so guilty that I even forget to be mad at the kids for being the culprits in the first place. I make a pact with myself that tomorrow it will be different. I will be more tolerant, understanding, calm, collected, even-tempered, but I know deep inside that the minute I am disrespected I will have the tendency to yell again. Why, oh why is parenting this difficult?!

It's not that I like to yell, or that I don't try to calmly speak to my kids at first, but when I do that they hear the nasal "mwa mwa" sound like in a *Charlie Brown* cartoon when adults are speaking. Basically, "Whatever, Mom. We know you are there physically but we are not going to hear you until you yell at us."

James 1:19 says, "Be quick to listen, slow to speak, and slow to get angry." It is perfect advice (of course it is, because it is from God), but when my hot European blood starts boiling—when my kids try to have the last word as they are walking away from me, or when they are fighting, sneering, faulting each other, bickering and badgering back and forth—my nerves become agitated like a washing machine on spin cycle, and my yelling erupts automatically.

And what exactly am I supposed to do when I am driving and my two kids are in the back seat blaming each other with "He touched me!" and "No I didn't! She's lying!" then kicking, all the while I am buckled in tightly in my driving seat not being able to stop the madness? You guessed it . . . I yell again, because they have just pushed all my buttons like those in an elevator being pressed all at once by some naughty kid, and then my brain locks up and verse James 1:19 goes out the window and I become *fast to speak and very quick to get angry.*

Please tell me you are identifying with me on this, even just a little bit, or you either have perfect children, or you have a strong hold on patience, or I am completely crazy! I have heard it said that parenting usually identifies who you are before you had children. In other words, if you are a patient person, parenting will amplify your patience, or if you are an affectionate person, then parenting will produce excess flow of affection. The latter is true in my case, but patience, on the other hand, does not come naturally to me. I am effervescent, full of love and passion, which makes me a loving but reactive person and parent. It is difficult for me to remember to be patient and calm in a frustrating situation because I tend to rev up like a Ferrari engine with instant ignition of anger.

I do strive and pray to be more mild-tempered, collected in manner and full of understanding and wisdom. James 3:17 says, "The wisdom that comes from heaven is first of all pure. It's also peace loving, gentle at all times, and willing to yield to others." These "others" also include our children, so I now I pray to God before I even get out of bed, to give me wisdom, patience, understanding, to make me aware of my anger, to slow me down in my reactions, and to fully prepare my mind as a parent. Proverbs 16:21 is fully memorized: "The wise are known for their understanding, and instruction is appreciated if well presented." And that is the key to any discipline: the way in which it is applied can lead to positive or inflammatory results.

God commands us in various places in the Bible to discipline our children. Why? Because He knows that we are sinners in need of daily correction. Proverbs 13:24 clearly states that "If you refuse to discipline your children, it proves that you don't love them." But that doesn't mean I have to constantly yell at them to get my desired result. Yelling is an ineffective way to discipline my children. It can be damaging to the parent-child relationship, to their ability to approach me as their confidant, as it may instill fearful reservation in creating intimacy and trust between us. I really don't want that to happen. My happiest moments are when my son shares with me his thoughts and worries while we lick popsicles on a hot porch, or when my daughter trusts me with very important questions too mature for her age, like what will happen when we die, what is heaven like, why did God allow poor people . . . I want our kids to call us first when they have good or bad news, and our home to be the place they first run to in any situation.

Parenting is tough and it never ends, and it becomes harder depending on the season we are in, baby stage, preschool, middle-school, teen years, and even their adulthood. Our worried parent hearts hope that our hard work will pay off. I pray that my kids, despite all my parenting flaws, will be fully prepared to lead healthy, wise, dedicated, effective God-centered lives.

Of course, it is impossible to *never ever* yell at our children, because we are all sinners, full of faults, but personally I have to make a conscious effort to not yell (as much), because it fosters more arguing, and my screaming will only lead to my kids becoming yellers themselves. So when I feel a yell welling up in my throat, I choose to leave the room, say a quick prayer (*Lord, please give me patience and wisdom*), then I take a deep breath to calm myself, and let God lead the way, trusting that He will guide my thoughts and actions when parenting my two children.

Chapter 3

Did Jesus Wear Nike Sandals?

Brand is not a product, that's for sure; it's not one item. It's an idea, it's a theory, it's a meaning, it's how you carry yourself . . .
—Kevin Plank, CEO of Under Armor

It is probably hard for my kids having an immigrant mother. Not only do they hear the inevitable adage "back in my day" (met with rolling eyes), but they also hear "back when I was growing up in Eastern Romania" tales of hardship.

My middle schooler is apparently experiencing chuckles and smirks for wearing plain white socks to school. Since it is a magnet school, they wear a uniform, so I thought there wouldn't be anything to compare or covet in the realm of clothes. But kids found a way to laugh at "just" plain white socks without a brand name etched at the top of the sock. "Nike" brand socks, particularly, will grant approving nods. All I have to say to that is "Good grief!" Really? Why? I wish I knew how to answer these questions, but all I can think about is that it's in our human nature to compare, to desire to belong and have what others promote as exciting and as "must-haves."

My son really wants Nike socks, Nike shoes, and my daughter has to have an American Girl doll, because all her friends at school have them. What's a parent supposed to do? The logical mode of action is not to give into the brands of clothes and dolls, thus teaching the kids humility, and contentment with what they have. But even at my age I felt the peer pressure from other parents, gave in and fed the brand-name frenzy by spending one hundred dollars on a doll (even though she already had two other "not up to cool code dolls"). I also bought trendy logo socks so my son wouldn't be made fun of anymore. Did I do the right thing? Probably not.

Honestly, I feel ill-equipped to address all the expensive labels, brands, and popular trendy fashions. And so, inevitably, my kids will hear my immigrant story.

I grew up in a very modest way, not having many nice things, and not realizing that there were nicer things to want or covet. As a society we did not have any availability to any trendy anything! We wore uniforms to school that looked exactly the same, down to the white socks, and we all bought our play clothes from the same neighborhood retail store, and played with similar toys and dolls. Brands were nonexistent, as were regular electricity, regular hot water, and white soft toilet paper. If we were lucky, the government allotted us hot water one day a week for a couple of hours. I showered quickly that one day in precious lukewarm water, and my mother heated it in aluminum pots the rest of the week and I wore lots of deodorant! (I know!) But that's just the way my life was. The very first time I took a long shower was at seventeen years of age in my father's house in Canada. It was hot, excessive, and it felt like paradise! Same went for the softest, plushiest toilet paper I had ever seen or touched. Mine, growing up was brown, rough, and scratchy, like sandpaper! It amazed me to see all the advertisements on this rudimentary necessity. Wow, double ply!

I try to impress on my children how privileged they are to live in such an abundant country, and how thankful they have to be every day, for the food in their tummies, hot showers, and fluffy toilet paper. I still don't take for granted the cushy feel, as I quickly evoke an otherwise bristly contact!

My children's favorite story is when my uncle Mihai from Romania came home to his mother's house (my grandmother), pouty and desolate. "What happened?" my grandma asked my aunt. "No one ask him any questions. We wanted to buy a blue car instead of a white one. They were out of blue ones."

Growing up in Romania everyone drove the exact model of car called *Dacia*. Since there were no other choices, the only thing left to the buyer's decision was the color of the car. I know this may sound weird but that was the reality back then. So my uncle had to live with a plain white car instead of his coveted blue!

Romans 12:2 says, "Do not be conformed to this world, but be transformed by the renewal of your mind, that by testing you will discern what is the will of God, what is good and acceptable and perfect" (ESV). God knows we are obsessive creatures, easily infatuated with pretty things, and immediately caught up in the trance of worldly offerings. That is exactly why He left us His guidance in verses like these. It is alright to partake of this world, just not to become slaves to it. I am not saying that brand-name clothes are not to be worn at all, because most likely they are very well made, with high quality and intended to last longer, so therefore we must pay more for them. It makes perfect sense from an entrepreneurial point of view to create beautiful quality workmanship, and supply and demand will determine how popular these name brands will become.

I, too, am guilty of a certain name-brand captivation. For the longest time, I referred to my boots as "I can't find my UGGS"; as opposed to "I can't find my boots." That's what they are after all—coverings for my feet, purposed to keep me warm and dry in the cold season—but I liked wearing them knowing that most women will undoubtedly lower their gaze to the back of the deliciously chocolate-brown sheepskin coverings and search for the popular logo. I felt confident that when other women will visually scan my boots, I will come up as a "match found" for belonging to the class of popular and accepted.

It should not matter what kind of logo I wear, but somehow it does even at my age. I think it's a pride issue, a vanity issue, and a fear issue. I feel pride because I am perceived as wealthy enough to afford name brands; vanity because I must look good while wearing them, and then I fear I will be secretly judged and disapproved of. Crazy stuff, I know. Growing up, I conformed to not having any choices, and now I willingly celebrate conformity out of sheer infatuation and lack of brain cells! I should not wear something just because others are doing it. If I like something, I should buy it because I think it's cool or trendy for ME, not to be popular. After all, the word "popularity" comes from the Latin *popularis* which literally means "belonging to the people," or "being loved by the people." So then, what my children are trying to achieve in their quest to wear the latest trends and possess certain brand-name dolls, shoes, and socks, is to belong to each other . . . All it takes is for one "fancy" kid to dictate what the leading trend is, and the rest will follow in fear and self-doubt.

With companies increasingly targeting children as the easily influenced and impressionable sponges, we have to shout our parenting efforts even louder, and engrave the Word of God on our children's minds and hearts and, in that process, perhaps remind ourselves not to become susceptible to commercial manipulation. My daughter inevitably said to me, "Mom, I love your UGGs, Can I have UGGs too?" Would it even occur to her to want them if I didn't make such a big deal about wanting a pair myself? After all, they were on *my* Christmas list . . . *Well . . . do as I say, honey, not as I do, for Mommy is not teaching you any valuable lessons!* I mean, did Jesus wear designer sandals, like *"Made by Joseph"* brand . . . Obviously not! I think that even in biblical days beautiful clothes mattered, but Jesus—although He has nothing against us having creativity and fashion sense—wants us to be more concerned with our character, and less preoccupied with comfort and appearance.

I tell my two children, as often as I can, not to derive their identity and self-worth from peer pressure of wearing the latest name brands and popular logos. Yes, they may be better quality, but that is not primarily why the kids wear them. The pressure to fit in is enormous on all kind of levels, especially in middle school and high school, so the last thing I want is for my kids to be bullied or isolated for not having a certain "check" mark on their shoes, or clothes, or for not having front teeth showing on their dolls (which is apparently how you can tell the expensive name-brand doll from the ordinary one). I was honestly about to paint in some front teeth myself when I found out how much I had to spend!

Dr. Seuss wrote, what I consider, a very profound book called *The Sneetches,* in which the star-bellied sneetches claim themselves better and superior because they in fact possess stars on their bellies. As a result the plain-bellied sneetches feel inferior and depressed, moping about with low self-esteem, feeling unwanted, disliked, and basically shunned.

Eventually, they are tempted to imprint stars on their bellies using clever machinery. As a result, all the sneetches now look exactly the same, but that in itself creates envy, and the duel of star bellies continues until they realize that it does not matter who has what!

It. Is. Stupid.

And so it goes with the popular name brands. If eventually all of the kids wear the exact name brands, they will get tired, bored, and frustrated with the whole thing. Spending precious energy on such venial, insignificant preoccupations can only lead to discontentment, depression, self-loathing, and feeling bullied.

"Who cares!" I tell my kids. And they say, "We do, Mom, because other kids care, so then we have to care as well!" "No, you don't!" I tell them. "If you look to God for guidance in all that you do, and pray for God to remove your temptations and desires, then He will. He just wants to see that you are not concentrating on the wrong things in life. God will convict you of the right emotions and decisions. He will provide opportunities for you to see and understand that all these fixations on name brands, logo crazes, and popularity do not matter in the forming of a godly character." I am certain that it sounds like blah-blah preaching against the adverse façade of belonging and fitting in, but I keep at it, and do what God commands me to do as I parent: "Train up a child in the way he should go; even when he is old he will not depart from it" (Proverbs 22:6 ESV).

After weeks of prayer that God would remove their desire of popular brands, my children finally became convicted. My son said, "Mom, I don't want you to buy me name-brand socks. I will wear my white ones. I don't care about what others think anymore." My daughter doesn't even play with her expensive front-toothed doll as much. A new occupation has taken over, a creative one, and I am happy to see their focus shift on worthier interests. We even started our own daily Bible study, where we look up Scriptures pertaining to our daily living. We recently discussed Mark chapter 12 in which Jesus was frustrated with the Pharisees only carrying about their outward appearance, wearing fancy robes and desiring popularity, and their hearts were corrupt with greed and deceit. I told the kids that Jesus dressed very modestly on purpose as to promote humble attitudes. People are easily seduced by luxury, but Jesus wanted to set an example on how we must stay focused on what's really important: being kind, giving, helpful, generous, and humble. We are not to stand out through brand-name clothes, but shine through our Christlike living. With God's help, my husband and I are trying to nurture our children's beliefs and attitudes, and pray they will become strong, faithful, and confident in their godly identity. Some evenings as I see them sleeping, I want to scoop my kids up and keep them safe and close, and not let them face the future, for I don't know what it may bring . . .

This makes me think of the movie *Finding Nemo*, when Marlin the clown fish is full of guilt over breaking the promise to his son of "never letting anything happen to him." Dory, the wise fish, explains to him, "You can't never let *anything* happen to him. Then nothing would ever happen to him." Life wouldn't be exciting. Yes, my kids, like most kids, will face bullying, challenges, brand-name pressures, frustrations, disappointments, and as much as I want to protect them and coddle them from all these things, I cannot. I must not.

Risk and courage are beautiful, rewards are exciting, God's wisdom and guidance are amazing and fulfilling, and I am blessed to be here and guide my children through their trials as they both inevitably reach out and grab handfuls of life.

Chapter 4

Mirror, Mirror, Are We Clear?!

Loving your body ONLY when it's in perfect shape, is like loving your kids ONLY when they're well-behaved.

—Picturequotes.com

High school can be very difficult, especially when you are from a different country, don't speak the language, and have no friends. That was exactly my situation when I was seventeen years old. I had swim class (as part of gym curriculum), when I caught three girls looking at me in the girls locker, sharing whispers, and then out came long laughter, followed by more mocking looks in my direction.

There they were in their artificial tan glory, the mean girls, with long bleached hair, cloaked in their exclusive bubble of skillful hostility. And then there was I . . . showing up for class with white "goose-bumped" skin, hairy legs, and red velvet boots. (Hold on, I will explain. I know it's hard to picture this.)

The red boots were the last gift my mother gave me before I moved to Canada to live with my father I had never met. I didn't own flip-flops, so I wore the only thing that was familiar to me. I know reading this may conjure up some shock or laughter, surely nonplussed by the disturbing image of red velvet boots, white skin, and hairy legs. Yes, I agree, not a good combo, and be sure that my early immigrant days in school still give me nightmares. So, then you ask, why didn't I shave my legs before swim class? Because my mother brought me up to love myself just the way God made me, which sounds noble and beautiful in theory, but she forgot to mention that we are all born in a fallen state, mine being—among other things—my hair abundance. It looked awesome on my head, but not when it reflected on my legs. And to think that all my turmoil, the low self-esteem, the knee highs in the middle of scorching summers, could have been avoided by a simple, glorious razor . . . Seriously, hairy legs should be covered by medical insurance as a deformity to one's body, as a harmful, emotionally and socially disturbing infirmity, and therefore obliterated by what would otherwise be elective, expensive laser hair removal!

So, then, as fallen state would have it, my sweet eight-year-old daughter, came home from school the other day and said, "Mommy, a girl from school told me I have really hairy legs. She showed me her legs, and she doesn't have any hair on them. Then other girls came to look at my hair, and I had the most . . ." Poor girl . . . I imagined her slender beautiful legs on display as her classmates came over with a magnifying glass inspecting a rare specimen! Oh, mirror, mirror on the wall, she's like her mother after all!

I was afraid to ask, but did anyway, "Did they laugh at you, honey?" Thankfully, they had not, but my daughter wanted to know why she had so much hair on her legs, while her friends had so little. *Well, sweetheart, that far-removed, but ever-so-present tiny "hairy" gene from your great-great-great-grandmother's side, sneaked in there and blossomed on my legs and now on yours!* Didn't quite say it this way to my darling girl, but I did explain to her how I had the same issue growing up, and how lucky for us to be alike in so many ways. She looked at me, undecided, with eyes wavering with conflict—me waiting with my stomach in knots to see if my encouraging words were convincing enough—until a smile borne of assurance and relief sprang on her innocent lips. *Phew! It worked*, I thought to myself, but as she walked away, she spun on her heels and announced: "I want to shave my legs!"

Well, there you go. She knows I shave my legs, so naturally she wants to do the same thing. I convinced her to wait until this coming summer, so now I have that decision waiting for me.

And this is just the beginning of entering the realm of body issues as it is a constant issue for our girls, be it elementary years or high school and beyond. The other day I learned from a television segment the matter concerning a certain "thigh gap," and a certain "bikini bridge." It's not enough to "just" be thin anymore (as if that wasn't tormenting and obsessive already), but apparently there is a new "improved" way of achieving a perfect body. Okay, so allow me to explain the "thigh gap" first. According to an internet definition, a "thigh gap" is the "gap between the thighs when standing with the back upright and the left and right knees are touching each other." Teen girls were explaining during this television interview how they consider themselves fat without these exalted traits. According to these girls, it is a craze right now to achieve this nonsensical gap as if their lives depend on it. They falsely perceive the thigh gap as the only way to have attractive thighs and legs. As a result they submit themselves to all kind of diets—starving diets, all juicing diets, stupid diets—just to achieve this blasted gap! Now, let me introduce you to the latest "upgrade": the "bikini bridge." This is basically "the bridge, or the space that forms when a bikini bottom suspends across a woman's hip bones, better seen when laying down, thus creating a bridge that connects to the hip bones" (internet definition). Say what?! I had to read it a few times to wrap my head around it. An exhausting definition, in my opinion.

As women, as parents to daughters, we must do something about this. As if life isn't challenging enough to try to mold proper characters, to teach our kids to be good, kind, sincere, loving, giving, and helpful, to ignore peer pressure, be compassionate, modest and so forth . . . Now, I have to worry about my daughter listening to this insanity, and hope she won't fall prey to its influence.

Personally, as a forty-two-year-old woman, who leads a somewhat healthy lifestyle, I do not possess either a thigh gap or a bikini bridge. Maybe I did when I was a four years old! We all have different genetic makeups and it's meant that way by God probably for the sake of beautiful variety. Psalm 139:13 assures us: "You made all the delicate, inner parts of my body, and knit me together in my mother's womb. Thank you for making me wonderfully complex! Your workmanship is marvelous—how well I know it." I know for a fact that God did not make a mistake in giving some of us thigh gaps, bikini bridges, or hairy legs, and to some fleshy, voluptuous legs, and smooth hairless skin.

We are who we are, so let's pray that we accept and love our bodies, and that our young girls do the same. It is absurd that our girls have to assault their intellect with such hen-witted, foolish concerns. WHO CARES! I know it's easy to say this when perhaps your child is suffering with body issues from not possessing these contrived, self-imposed features, but poor self-image is a major issue in our society. It is incredibly difficult to shelter our teens and ourselves from the incessant exposure of the media which is consumed with auctioning outward beauty in an unrealistic and skewed way. There are endless commercials advertising a litany of diets and ways to ensure ourselves skinny and fit, ready to be adored and secretly envied by those who don't have enough "will" or "self-discipline" to survive and conquer this insatiable, exhausting race to achieving the "perfect" body!

First Peter 3:3 instructs us, "Don't be concerned about outward beauty that depends on fancy hairstyles, expensive jewelry, or beautiful clothes. You should be known for the beauty that comes from within." Notice that it doesn't say to not have these outward beauty adornments at all, but simply to not allow ourselves to be ruled by them or make it the focus of our attention. I agree that is hard to convince my eight-year-old daughter of this biblical wisdom, but when she is looking in the mirror scrutinizing herself, I assure her that she is made in God's image, and she's perfect just the way she is. Unfortunately, she is using the word "fat" to describe her skinny legs and thighs. My heart winces with despair, as panic surges and I chastise myself as a parent: "How could I let this happen?! Where, when, how, why, from whom is she learning this falsehood?" Why does it occur to her to even think of her body image at such a young age? Are the other girls at school doing the same thing? Am I to blame? Am I using the word "fat" to bully myself when I am not aware of it? Possibly, because I, too, am caught in the wicked current of self-criticism when involved in conversation with my women friends, referring to our beloved bodies in ways God would disapprove of, while my young daughter with innocent years is playing nearby . . .

When I was a teen, breast size was definitely a topic of discussion, but now since we are able to adjust that, are we supposed to have flesh removed to reveal a gap? It is ridiculous to even address this as a topic of discussion, but apparently I have no choice but alarm myself with these worries for the sake of my daughter, OUR daughters. And by the way, even my middle school son complains that his thighs are too big and too "meaty," and that his friends are making fun of his white "meaty" legs! Excuse me for a bit while I go scream in my closet!

Okay, so what are we to do to equip our kids with healthy body images and with nonvolatile wisdom, in order to resist falling prey to dangerous stigmas like "bikini bridges," "thigh gaps," "meaty legs," "hairy legs," "fat legs," or who knows what other beef-brained and obtuse body referrals.

First Samuel 16:7 clearly states about a person, "Do not consider his appearance, or height, for I rejected him. The LORD does not look at the things man looks at. Man looks at the outward appearance, but the LORD looks at the heart" (NIV). This is the foundation we must assure our children of. Like any subjective mother, I think my daughter is so beautiful, and I marvel at her outward appearance all the time, but lately I try to refrain from complementing her beauty, and instead, I commend her for being kind, smart, giving, considerate, loving, and compassionate. I call her my "solution finder" because she loves solving any problems, and her face lights up at her nickname.

I also began limiting television watching for the kids, no commercials allowed, no popular magazine exposure with unrealistic, airbrushed bodies of models and celebrities. I am not trying to shelter my girl from the reality of our society, but teach her to occupy her thoughts with meaningful, godly interests. We will always be the best at what we do the most, so if she concerns herself with healthy, wholesome focuses, she will continually absorb nutritious, virtuous qualities, and hopefully not give foolish body topics any worth. Then, she will find acceptance and identity in what Jesus has to say about her: "Instead it should be that of your inner self, the unfading beauty of a gentle and quiet spirit, which is of great worth in God's sight" (1 Peter 3:4 NIV).

It may seem excessive to tackle this topic, but idealistic expectations on body image can be very damaging to our girls. It can cause them perhaps succumb to the perils of anorexia, bulimia, and emotionally assaulting diseases (like depression), and ultimately acquire an abnormal, harmful view of themselves and their beautiful God-tailored bodies. God doesn't expect us to constantly eat unhealthy processed foods and become overweight, but instead to treat our bodies as a temple and honor Him with it by staying healthy: "So whether you eat or drink, or whatever you do, do all to the glory of God" (1 Corinthians 10:31). As parents, we can role-model regular exercise, embrace outdoor activities, and go swimming, fishing, or running together. Many of my friends run 5Ks and triathlons with their kids, thus teaching them to stay active. Any local YMCA can help you with that. We can keep our kids off screen time by giving them house chores, promoting responsibility and self-discipline. They can also volunteer through church, go on mission trips to help others, tutor other kids, and be part of youth groups and Bible studies. When our son participated in an afterschool tutoring program for underprivileged children, he started to pray regularly for those he met. He was filled with compassion and eager to serve more.

God gave us all a beautiful, precious, and challenging existence. Yes, we may struggle with having hairy legs, fleshy legs, with fitting in, with accepting our bodies for what they are, but we are not alone in this. We have the Holy Spirit and the Bible to sustain and guide us as parents, as children, as human beings.

Our daughters and sons deserve the very best of our attention, guidance, and protection from the many temptations of this world, so we must impress on them from a young age how and where to find beauty and true worth. I do hope that when my daughter and son look in the mirror, they will have a clear understanding of the godly images reflecting back at them.

Chapter 5

Somebody Help Me!

Put it there if it weighs a ton. That's what the father said to his youngest son. As long as you and I are here, put it there.

—Paul McCartney, "Put It There"

Agh!!! I can't take middle school anymore! My son comes home every day brooding, sulking, and pensive. He looks at me sometimes as if he has never seen me before. Definitely enrolled in the Space Cadet Academy, he has a hard time focusing, making eye contact, and answering any of my "interesting" questions. I ask, "So . . . how was your day, who did you have lunch with, did you learn anything, how did you do on your math test, do you like that girl?" I get savant answers: "Good, can't remember, I guess, fine, I don't want to talk about it." Phew, elaborate day! I hope I don't become an inconvenience to his existence!

"Okay . . . Well, I made your favorite dessert for after dinner. Isn't that exciting?"

"Yep."

He drops his jacket at the front door—actually, no, he hangs it up (so, I'm doing something right as a parent)—and goes to his room to do his homework. The door shuts closed; an impenetrable force field. That went well. My heart squeezes in my chest, and now I know how Mary felt, when her son Jesus nonchalantly excluded her after she frantically searched for his whereabouts. What happened to my little boy? . . . Where did he go? . . . He has left the land of *Winnie the Pooh* (his favorite childhood movie), and he is claimed by a PG-13 movie filled with mystery and suspense, as I am flying by the seat of my pants. I don't quite know how to parent him through this difficult stage. He is having a hard time at school this year, especially socially. He feels he is not well liked, or that he is not popular at all. He claims through tormented eyes that certain boys say to him, "Nobody likes you," "Get away from me," "You're annoying." Why are boys so mean? I thought the "mean domain" belongs to the girls.

As he no longer has to climb on top of the counter to reach the cereal, I watch him as he quietly retrieves his desired sort, pours milk over it, and sits gently across from me with eyes down, silently chewing. There is so much sadness etched on his young face . . . I can see the weariness in the set of his shoulders. He shouldn't have to carry such burdens already, and yet I don't know how to make him see that none of this matters in the long scope of life, that these immature boys with menial attitudes are just that: immature. I want so much to walk up and hug him but I battle the urge, because that would freak him out for sure. Right now, at his age, I am told by seasoned parents, that I have to respect his personal space. He used to be the one seeking me out, climbing on my lap allowing me to caress his chocolate brown hair. (Sigh.) He may be on the brink of becoming a young man, but yet his childish features persist in his pillowy soft cheeks, his wavy lush hair, and his deep, copper-toned inquisitive eyes.

I love both my kids beyond reason, and I want so desperately to fix all that is hurting my son right now and all that makes him so unhappy, but I know that God never promised us a life without trials or pain. This is a season in his life he will have to find his way through, and so I have to let the growing up beckon as it may. Remember the scene in the famous movie *It's a Wonderful Life*, when little Zuzu's petals fell off her flower and she turns to her father pleading, "Paste it, Daddy"? Our kids look to us for help in their lives, and no matter how frustrated and difficult my son's school life is, all I can do is listen to him and turn his ears to God's wisdom.

"But, Mom, there is no one else to choose from at school. Everyone has friends but me!"

"I know it feels that way," I tell him. It is a small magnet school, but I remind him of God's assurance, "Son, trust the Lord with all your heart, in every aspect of your life because He really cares about what happens in your life." This is a combination of Proverbs 3:5-6 and 1 Peter 5:7.

"Surely, there are other boys whom no one reaches out to. Make friends with those boys," I advise him.

"Yes, but I have nothing in common with *those* guys. All they do is read, and they don't want to talk about anything cool, and I am a very social person!"

"A-ha, you don't feel like hanging out with those boys because they seem like outcasts, but Jesus would reach out to those who are lonely, and without company. Just try to make a difference in their lives, and God would bless you for it."

"Mom, I feel weird doing that."

"I know, but God is more interested in our character, in doing the right thing, more than in our comfort."

"What this means," I explain, "is that you can pray to God to provide new friends for you, friends with good, faithful hearts. Just have patience, stay focused on your school work, try to stay away from the 'popular' boys, and take a chance on other kids."

I read to him Isaiah 43:19: "Behold, I am doing a new thing; now it springs forth, do you not perceive it?"

"But, how do I deal with that heavy feeling, on my heart, when I first wake up? I really don't want to go to school . . ."

"Well, say a prayer, telling God you trust Him with your day, and then change your attitude, and smile wide until you feel yourself lighter and more positive." My son loves history so I bring the wise words of Abraham Lincoln into our conversation: "'Most folks are about as happy as they make up their minds to be.' I also have to make a conscious decision to think and be positive. It is hard some of the time."

"What do I say to the guys when they start saying mean things to me again?"

"Just because they say something, it doesn't make it true. They are also dealing with their own insecurities. They probably make others feel bad, so they can feel better about themselves. Pray for those boys for you don't know what kind of home life they lead."

"I just don't get it, Mom. They used to be nice to me last year but now they choose not to be, it makes me so angry! I have no friends, Mom!"

"They sound like frenemies." (I try to keep up with the latest lingo that defines someone who is both a friend and an enemy.) My son rolls his eyes.

"It is hard to be a Christian . . ."

"Yes it is. I am proud of you for doing the right thing and not joining in and saying mean things as well. It takes courage to be godly."

At bedtime I read to him one of my favorite verses: "The LORD your God is with you, the Mighty Warrior who saves. He will take great delight in you . . . [and] rejoice over you with singing" (Zephaniah 3:17 NIV).

Now, do not think for a single minute that all of the above took place in a single fluid conversation, while we ate ice cream on the porch swing. Not at all. I just compiled it all for the sake of this chapter, and to be easier for you to understand the wisdom of God's Word in relation to my son's predicaments. All my outreach took place over the course of a few months, and not every day, but in bits and pieces, here and there, whenever I perceived an opportunity. Since my boy is not as open and available as he used to be, I tried not to freak him out by sitting him down and solemnly announce: "Let's see how we can fix all this for you." He would probably run the other way. All kids are different, with intrinsic dispositions, and at this stage in his life, I had to adopt a different strategy. He loves to skateboard, play Xbox, listen to music, play guitar, and read sci-fi books, so I decided to learn more about his interests even though it took time and, honestly, at times had to fake my level of enthusiasm.

I learned Xbox multiplayer terms abbreviations like 10m (Ten Man), 2M2H (Too much to handle), Ace (solo winner), AFK (away from the keyboard), and my favorite, Baller (cool person). I asked my son if I could play some games with him and tried using these terms trying to appear cool, but I know I ended up sounding like a dork. But it's okay because by doing that it gave me an entry into my son's thoughts and in between games he opened up about his struggles and that's partly when I used the Word of God to advise him.

Also I tried skateboarding, not before I "Wikipediaed" some information. I learned that the board part is actually called a "deck," that the top part is "grip tape," that "air" refers to riding in the air, and that an "Ollie" is a jump that happens by popping the tail of the board to the ground. I used my right foot to lead on purpose so when my son told me I was doing it wrong, I said, "Yeah, I know. It's called a 'goofy-foot.'" I think I impressed the pants off of him! He didn't share anything profound with me while skateboarding in front of our house, but *our time together increased the probability of future discussions.*

I started showing much interest in his favorite music, which actually became some of my favorite as well and he was more than happy to download his albums onto my iPod too. I read the book he was reading simultaneously so we could discuss it together, and slowly all of my incipient efforts resulted in the two of us getting closer, and thus providing a climate where he can feel comfortable sharing his burdens with me.

Like I said before, it didn't work like magic overnight, but I felt I was "losing" my son to false beliefs and false agreements he was making to himself about himself. Only God can shed truth and light over us. I know it is important to our kids how their friends and peers perceive them, as it is still important to grown adults. I wanted to fit in, be important, and be popular without feeling inferior to my peers. Remember the mean girls that laughed and made fun of me and my red boots? I felt so alone in a new country, with no friends, no family that knew me, not speaking the language. I told our son that I get it, I really do, but all we can do is turn to God and He will guide us through. I also know that is hard for him to compute all this into his twelve-year-old mind, especially since he takes everything to heart, he is very impassioned, and easily affected by everything in his life (like his momma!). We do share the same visceral grasp on life. Instead of shrugging our shoulders, we store our feelings tightly inside, like a squirrel stores nuts, and keeps them there until hopefully things make sense.

Former First Lady Eleanor Roosevelt said, "No one can make you feel inferior without your consent." I just love this so much, so I keep pounding the parenting pavement, never letting go, never giving up, and continually on my knees praying for both our children, for God to give them wisdom, guidance, and assurance in all that they do. I have to remind myself that we all went to school, so we all had to survive peer pressure, mean words, hostile people, lonely days, friends that moved away, eating lunch alone, fighting back tears as others laughed in contempt, but all of it has passed and gotten absorbed into the realm of yesteryears. Some people will always shock us with their bitter, callous ways, but some will surprise us with their goodness, kindness, love, and acceptance.

Yes, my son is in middle school right now—with many issues, hormonal changes, fears, frustrations, insecurities, desires, expectations—and there is teen land coming up with its own set of challenges, like girl issues, driving worries, and then I have to do it all again with our daughter. But that is okay for as long as we have the Word of God on our side we say: "Bring it on! We can do this parenting thing!"

"I can do all things through Christ, who gives me strength" (Philippians 4:13), is my mantra and I hold on to it for dear life!

Chapter 6

"What . . . That's All I Got?!"

Where does stuff go when it dies, does it go to stuff heaven?
—George Carlin, comedian

One of my fondest childhood memories is of Christmas holidays. Every year we celebrated Christmas at my grandparents' house in a small Romanian village. I always looked forward to riding the train in the winter, looking at the snow-covered trees running by as I anticipated my grandpa waiting for me at the train station with the sleigh he had built himself. My grandma was baking sweet cheese buns and walnut loaves, and the air was filled with scents of nutmeg and mulled cider. Maybe it's odd but I never think of presents I received or even presents I gave. Christmas was not about getting stuff. My memories are strictly redolent of my grandma's house, the food, and of our family laughing and trying to figure out where everybody was going to sleep!

My kids are spoiled rotten, to tell you the truth. They both make lists of what they want for Christmas, and every year I search long and hard to get them what they want, and even get them more stuff that wasn't even on their list! Why? Because I simply can't help myself! I get wrapped up in the flurry of pretty colors, decorations, sparkly globes, shiny tinsel . . . I see my neighbor's trunk open filled with bags, as I snoop through my window wondering what did she get her kids that I didn't get mine. Ridiculous, right?

First John 2:16 says, "For all that is in the world, the desires of the flesh and the desires of the eyes and pride in possessions is not from the

Father but is from the world." This verse rings more true in our today's society which suffers with possession obsession, and desires for instant gratification. We are bombarded with ads even as we drive our cars, so it is difficult for our children to be thankful for what they already have. The problem is that I, the parent, am also caught up in the possession obsession whirlwind, because I have the freedom to "see it" and "get it." I am obsessed with watching HGTV makeovers of kitchens and bathrooms and yards and whole new houses. I get a certain covetous buzz, dreaming with my eyes open for what I would change about my house, and how quickly can I move somewhere else. I stare, thinking what wall can I take down, what new color should I paint my kitchen cabinets, how am I going to afford a farm sink (they cost as much as a mortgage payment!). How can I change my house—make it "better," more exciting, more fashionable? I imagine choosing a different décor, even if it is as small as a new salt shaker or a burnt orange vase, or whatever "needful" thing I perceive I have to have, all the while ushering in discontentment and frustration. Who needs all these dissatisfied thoughts?!

Frankly, I am very surprised at myself considering I come from humble beginnings, growing up in a former Communist country, where we had to be thankful we even had certain foods on our table. I grew up with many hardships, where after school, instead of watching TV (we didn't have one actually), or playing the latest electronic device (laugh out loud!), I had to stand in long queues for basic necessities like milk, flour, sugar, and bread. Limited quantities of meat arrived maybe once a month at the local butchery, as I stood in line for hours just to be given the allotted portion. It was tiring, annoying, inconvenient, and frustrating, but I had to be grateful to have made it before the door shut in my face and the sign read: "Out of meat." Also, hot water was a commodity, and only allowed to flow once a week, and electricity was cut off every evening for many hours. I did my homework by candlelight, and shivered under cold showers!

We live in an abundant country with access to all our hearts' and credit cards' desire, and it has to be a constant and conscious choice to not get sucked in into the copious vortex of opulence and entitlement. I was watching a television show a few weeks ago that dealt with overindulging our children. The show featured parents that did not know where the financial limit is when it came to having birthday parties for their kids. One mother spent over three thousand dollars on her son's eighth birthday party! The event was fully catered, and gifts were expensive, elaborate, and superabundant. When asked why she resorts to such extreme, she said it is because she sees other parents outdo each other all the time. Thus it became a stressful competition between parents in the neighborhood and she felt like she had to keep up. As I was watching I thought, *What in the world will she do next year, and what kind of message is she sending to her son through all of this?*

I am also familiar with a particular sixteen-year-old who asked for a very expensive sound system for her room. She loved music so she expected top-of-the-line speakers, and an expensive CD player (obviously not a recent story!). This was a tremendous financial sacrifice for her parents, and so they felt since this was a costly present, that they didn't have to get her anything else for her birthday. On the big day, the eager parents presented their daughter with the most anticipated gift. As they breathlessly awaited her elated response, she exclaimed: "Wow, I knew you were going to get me this. It's cool and all . . . but is this all I got for my birthday, one present?"

The nineteenth-century author Oscar Wilde said that "the worst thing in life is not having what you want and having what you want." The more we give our children, the more they feel entitled. So then, why do I fret so much over giving my own kids exactly what they ask for Christmas and their birthdays? Perhaps is it because I am trying to compensate for the things I didn't get as a child, but as I said before I cannot even begin to recall what I lacked in presents under the Christmas tree, because family togetherness meant more. All I can think of is that it is not in our human nature to automatically yield with our hearts first, but more with our eyes. God knows that about us, so in His goodness, He anticipated our fleshly desires, by leaving us His wisdom in Matthew 6:19–21:

> "Do not store up treasures here on earth, where moths eat them and rust destroys them, and where thieves break in and steal. Store your treasures in heaven, where moths and rust cannot

destroy. . . . Wherever your treasure is, there the desires of your heart will also be."

We have to prepare our children to fight the temptation of accumulation, of wanting and then wanting some more, and our best tool is to guide them early in life to God's Word, to remind them of being grateful, to bring awareness of the ones less fortunate, and involve them in serving their community and giving generously as much as possible.

I read the following anonymous quote:

Ask your children two questions this Christmas. First: "What do you want to give others for Christmas?" Second: "What do you want for Christmas?" The first fosters generosity of heart and outward focus. The second can breed selfishness if not tempered by the first.

I love these wise words. Basically, it is more of a blessing to give than to receive, and the sooner our families as a whole get addicted to giving the better it will be. Christmas should be about the birth of Jesus Christ, and it is very difficult nowadays to keep that in the forefront of our minds, especially for children who instinctively become enamored with setting up the Christmas tree, with picking and shaking the presents under it with much glee and anticipation.

It is very natural for all of us to be expectant of gift giving and receiving, to be caught up in the euphoria of inexplicable Christmas joy, anticipating family togetherness, laughter, flurry of morning hugs and kisses, and bright-colored wrapping scattered about. These are wonderful memories in our lives. On the other hand, we also must consciously think of the less fortunate, the ones that spend the holidays alone, forgotten, perhaps unwanted, buried by struggles, and heavy hearts. Taking our kids to homeless shelters, volunteering to hand out presents to those in need, going to nursing homes to hand our homemade Christmas cards and reading from the Bible to the lonely elderly, filling up boxes for the kids in underdeveloped countries via Operation Christmas Child are all tangible ways to bring our focus as a family off of ourselves and onto others.

Because of our fast rhythm as a society, because of the age of increased social media, I believe, our kids are in danger of becoming more isolated physically and emotionally, their lifestyle more conducive to self-importance, self-involvement, and self-concern. We the parents have to make our children aware that there is a big suffering world outside of themselves. The shiny tinsel should fade away into the less important realm, and we must reveal great summits of compassion for all the destitute people around us. We need to change our young ones' attitudes from "What, that's all I got?" to "What else can I do for others?" I am the first one to admit that we do not do nearly enough as we should as a family, but when we do reach out and give of our time and resources, our kids are better behaved, our family has more harmony, we are less argumentative, more peaceful, more content. We are more like Christ and so, naturally, we feel more joy.

Jesus did say in Acts 20:35: 'It is more blessed to give than to receive'" (NIV). I need to read this verse basically every day, as my heart starts whining, and complaining. We try (notice I said *try*, for we don't always remember to do this), when our family is safely tucked around our dinner table, to share what we are each thankful for that day. It can be anything from provision of food, shelter, safety, health, good friends, finances, to having a sunny day to enjoy outside, great teachers at school, for laughter, to finding something we lost. This way, every day, the kids, Mom, and Dad are conscious toward appreciation of our lives and not taking anything for granted. In the end that's all we have, the very day we are in, endowed to us by the grace and love of God. "This is the day the LORD has made. We will rejoice and be glad in it" (Psalm 118:24). The sooner our children, understand, internalize, and practice this godly wisdom, the better they will be at wanting less and show contentment more—and that, in my humble opinion as a parent, is a monumental achievement.

Chapter 7

Train Wreck

When I am overwhelmed, you alone know the way
I should turn. (Psalm 142:3)

It is 6:50 in the morning—time to wake up and go through my predictable morning routine. First thing I do is turn the gas stove on and poach the regular egg whites (the only thing my daughter eats for breakfast). While the water heats up, I make a quick run to the bathroom, get dressed, and start preparing lunches. My son's light is on, as usual—he is getting ready for school. My husband is working in his office upstairs, and we have to leave now in fifteen minutes. My eight-year-old girl is still refusing to wake up, to the perpetual aggravation of her impatient and militantly on-schedule brother. He yells at her from the breakfast table, "You are such a lazy bum! Get up! We are never on time because of you!"

"Don't call your sister a lazy bum," I chime in as I piggyback her from the bed into the living room. My son is relentless, "Ugh! She needs to get dressed by herself. She's such a baby!"

"Shut up!" His sister is clearly wide awake now.

"Don't say shut up to your brother."

"But he is so mean to me!" she cries as crocodile tears flow down her cheeks.

"Oh, stop crying! It's so annoying! You're just trying to get me in trouble with your fake crying!"

"Kids, listen to your mother. Do as you are told." My husband is coming down the stairs, rushing and scanning around for any item he may forget before he leaves for work.

The kids kiss him goodbye as they promise, with an exchange of furtive and smirking looks, to be good for Mom. I am thankful that the patriarch has spoken; therefore, peace *should* be restored. It is 7:35 and it's now five minutes past our departure time.

"Let's goooooo!!!" The boy is growing impatient as he taps his foot really fast in increased agitation.

"Stop tapping your foot near my ear," his sister sneers at him as she fumbles with her shoelaces sitting on the floor.

"I can do whatever I want. *You* are the slowest person on the planet!"

"Mom, he is so mean!"

"Okay kids, let's just go. You can put your shoes on in the car. We are late."

My son chuckles in triumph, emboldened by my remark, which he perceives as Mom being on his side. He passes by his sister and bumps her with his backpack (hopefully not on purpose, but by now I am not sure). She hits him back. Provoking looks are sparking high and, instead of leaving out the open door, they start pestering each other back and forth, taunting each other with pokes, pinches, slaps on behinds, full-on body contact like a couple of German Shepherds.

I am literally in disbelief of the energy they possess half an hour into their day. I am desperately trying to think of a Bible verse that deals with love, affection, kindness, but cannot think of any. I am left flickering my frustrated gaze from one kid to another, watching them return each other's volley with such ambitious hostility. My nerves are smoldering high with smoke coming out of my ears (like the old cartoons). Brimful with aggravation, I decree a severe warning and tell them to get in the car. I battle the urge to lecture them, as I am deeply disappointed at their behavior and cinders of my anger are still very much alive! *Don't parent in anger,* I say to myself. So, I say nothing—the kids, clearly aware of the elevated tension, finally keep to themselves.

We start driving, and the engine light comes on. Now what!? That's all I need, for something to be wrong with the engine . . . Aghhh!! It's okay. I will deal with it later. I just want to get the kids to school on time. I apply my brakes for the red light at the end of my street and they grind heavily, giving out a loud roar, and the metal friction chokes my brakes as they barely grip underneath my foot, making the whole car shudder. My husband put new brake pads on my minivan the day before—the poor guy is working twelve-hour days—and I guess he put the brake pads on inside-out . . . I freak out, "Oh my goodness, the brakes are not working properly! Dear Jesus, please get us to school." I am driving slowly, potentially making us even later than I thought. The kids are having fun each time the car quakes, simulating (to them alone) an amusement park ride!

I put my emergency lights on and we are driving the best we can. My husband is coaching me over the phone to pump my brakes for now, and once I get the kids to school to not drive the car anymore. My white-knuckled fingers are clenching the steering wheel, trying not to betray a tiny smile as the kids still cheer in the background . . . Kids will be kids. (At least they are getting along right now.) I allow myself a tiny exhale, when the gas light comes on with an unexpected loud "ding" causing an anxiety jolt in the pit of my stomach. My morning is fantastic: the kids were uncontrollable, engine light is on, gas light is on, and my brakes are failing! Somebody, please muffle my scream!! It's only 7:57 in the morning and I feel exhausted. It feels like I've had a very long day already. At least we are at school three minutes before the doors close. Phew!

A scream of panic comes from the back seat, as my daughter starts to cry and guiltily says, "Mom, look at my feet . . ." I do, and so I see my girl wearing a boot on one foot and a tennis shoe on the other. Through frustrated tears, she explains that she felt so rushed this morning and stressed out by all the commotion with her brother, and hustled out the door, that she just did not realize that she put on two different shoes. Poor kid, honest mistake . . . I feel at fault somehow, because I am naturally the emotional shock absorber of the family. Now, I have to take her to the school office and explain her situation.

I am suddenly keenly aware that I do not have a bra on. Since I left the house in a hurry, and did not anticipate having to get out the car, I did not bother to get dressed for the day. This of course, shamelessly implies that this is my daily routine, but there it is, I admit it: I wake up, put leggings on and a long sleeve on top of my pajama T-shirt. For now, I have no choice but try to appease my bed hair by tossing it in a messy bun. I clutch my shirt across my chest as naturally as possible and we all walk into school together.

Conscious that I was holding my breath in tension, I exhale. *It's alright, I can do this. "It's just regular life with the lid pried off."* I read this in a book and it rings so true this morning.

The principal decides that my daughter will have to go to class "as she is" and that I may quickly go home and bring matching shoes. I really wanted to explain to her that I can't do that actually—that I had a tangled and complicated day already, with car brakes that don't work—but I realize all that is relevant to the school boss is to rectify my daughter's predicament. "Yes, ma'am. I will be back in fifteen minutes," I respond, not entirely sure how I will fulfill my promise.

I am one foot out the door as I hear my name spoken by the middle school guidance counselor, "Mrs. Hackett?"

"Um . . . Ye-es . . . ," I answer, as my heart winces inside its cage. This can't be good as I am invited to take a sit in her office. All I can think about, as my heart pounds with anticipation, is that I have to go "somewhere" and produce matching shoes. I feel like I am in trouble, with the door closing tight behind her, bringing back unwanted school memories. My cheeks are burning with anticipation, anxiety rising in my chest, so I clasp my cold sweaty hands in my lap. I have no idea what this is about.

"Mrs. Hackett, are you aware that your son has been emotionally bullied at school?"

Am I aware? What do you mean by THAT . . . that I am not an involved mother, that I am not interested in my son's life, that I am too busy to care? Yes, my son has had a rough year starting middle school, but we have been praying through it. Considering my morning so far, I filter everything through weak nerves.

"Yes, I am aware. My son tells me everything, every day," I assure her. "He is such a considerate young boy, so kind, funny, smart, and godly. He always tries to do the right thing, and this is a hard time in his life, not knowing how to fit in with the other more popular boys. He is such a faithful friend, if only those boys would realize what a fantastic human being he is."

I am erratic, expecting hormonal boys to "realize" anything of depth and importance, but I ramble on using the guidance counselor as my daily journal, telling her all about my morning and my frustration with the kids, as I start to cry profusely wiping snot and tears with my sleeve. She hands me a tissue as she rushes to close the other door that leads out to the main hallway where everybody can hear and see me. Poor woman, I bet she did not expect to encounter an overwhelmed, emotionally fluctuant mother this morning. However, she is listening with affection and kindness. She concurs that my son is a great kid, confused by middle school peer pressure, hormones lashing out in every direction, and—no way around it—this is just a season in his life. She will have a talk with him soon and, not to worry, she will keep me informed as the situation ensues. I apologize for my emotional release, and she pats me on the shoulder: "It's okay. You are a good mom. You care about your kid. It's normal." She seals our meeting with a smile and I am out the door.

What a train wreck of a day so far! It's only 8:30 a.m. and I've seen more action than most would in one whole day! Somehow, I feel responsible for the whole thing. Every chamber of my heart is filled with guilt and blame. I feel like I am a bad parent, making all the wrong decisions, at the wrong time; otherwise, if I was more patient, more in control, more mentally organized and more disciplined, none of this would have happened. It is irrational, I know, but I cannot help it. I literally feel like having a grown-up tantrum adorned with all the jumping up and down, laying on the ground, kicking my feet, screaming and crying for someone's attention. Of course I don't. (I'm not *that* crazy!) All the self-reproach bunches forward, pushing a surge of tears to fall down my face.

I am walking to my car, not sure what I am going to do next, as I see one of my best friends drive by. God is so good. I get in, and she listens with concern and compassion as I am unleashing all about my morning. What would we do without faithful friends? She comforts me with encouraging words, assuring me that train wreck mornings happen to everyone, including herself. She drives me to a nearby Target store and I buy new shoes for my girl. It's going to be alright. "When I am overwhelmed, you alone know the way I should turn" (Psalm 142:3). All of a sudden, I feel grateful for my "train wreck morning." God knew in advance of my troubled morning, so He sent me a friend at the perfect time. I feel so loved and looked after and I thank God for tangibly being there amid my problems.

I sure hope that any of you reading this identifies with me, or I will really feel like a crazy person! Please tell me you are nodding in "I know exactly how you feel" agreement, perhaps recognizing yourself in a version of this story.

Life will be life and it's going to do its thing, and although I am not quite ready to laugh out loud about my treacherous morning, I know one thing for sure: I will never ever leave my house without a bra on!

Chapter 8

Dehydrated Fruit Syndrome

Each of you should use whatever gift you have received to serve others, as faithful stewards of God, grace in its various forms. (1 Peter 4:10)

I have been on the *Today* show many times already, being interviewed by Matt Lauer regarding my books I have written and published so successfully.

"So, Roxana, you've never had any formal training as a writer. You didn't get your master's degree in literature, and yet you write so well and with such ease. I must say it's very impressive considering that English is not your first language. You're originally from Romania, right?"

"Matt, first of all, let me just say how grateful I am to be on the show again. Yes, I moved to North America when I was seventeen years old but writing has always been my passion. I even started my own dictionary compiled with words I love. Since I was younger my dream was to go to Oxford and study linguistics and literature."

I am wearing an embroidered pastel yellow linen dress with delicate white stitching to reflect an elegant but Bohemian look, my favorite. I feel comfortable and very happy in it. Matt picks up my book.

"So, the title in itself is hilarious: *When Are Your Parents Coming to Get You?* Explain a bit how you came to use this title."

"It was really my husband's idea. When our kids were little, he used to ask them, 'When are your real parents coming to get you?' and our kids would say 'Never!' and he would laugh and respond, 'Never?! Oh no!!!'

and they would all laugh and tickle each other. It was said as a way to reinforce how much in awe we are of these amazing kids being our own and what a privilege parenting really is."

"Well, I read it and laughed out loud a few times. I recommend this book to all parents out there. Thank you for coming, Roxana. Again, the book is called—"

"Mom! Mommmm! I need toilet paper! There's no more toilet paper! Mom!?"

My fantasy bubble got popped by the urgent call of providing a roll of toilet paper to my kid. Whenever I wash dishes I tend to slip into certain reveries, daydreaming about my own ambitions and imagine myself in different places in life. I have always been a creative human being, completely void of left-brain propensities, but entirely abundant in right-brain abilities. (Or so I think, anyway.)

When I was little I would sew clothes for my dolls, and took great interest in every detail of color and created "haute couture" doll outfits from my mother's old dresses. I used to memorize poems by Romanian writers and invite my mother's guests to sit and listen to my reciting. (I can see my husband now forming with his thumb and forefinger an "L" shape on his forehead, lovingly teasing of course!) I know it may sound "nerdy" of me but I think God has given me creative passion and artistic penchants. I just can't help myself. Recently, I read a great book called *The Artisan Soul: Crafting Your Life into a Work of Art* by Erwin Raphael McManus, author and founder of Mosaic Church in Los Angeles, in which he writes about human creativity and reclaiming our creative essence which we all actually possess in one way or another. Pastor McManus says, "We all need to create, to be a part of a process that brings to the world something beautiful, good and true, in order to allow our souls to come to life."[2] And you don't need to sculpt, paint, or write to be creative. It can be anything that percolates inside of you as a human being, a calling to something that fuels your passion.

I believe that, as parents, we sometimes "lose" our own selves, our own definition, into the fruitful but ever-so-demanding territory of parenting. I am not saying I don't love being a mother, but at the same time I don't cease to exist as an individual created by God in His image.

Pastor Erwin says, "He who is the Creator God is the creative God, and he created us in his image and likeness. He created us with imagination and curiosity, with the capacity to hope and dream."[3]

The truth is that no matter what I do throughout the day, the incandescent filament of creativity is always burning. It is on low, but nonetheless is there—present, pressing, and gnawing at my mind and soul, longing to fan into flames. There's a Taylor Swift song called "22" that goes, "I don't know about you but I'm feeling 22." Well in my case it goes, "I don't know about you, but I'm feeling 42!" That is because I am actually forty-two! I believe God expects me to write with transparency and passion, and to bring glory to Him in this way. So then, here I am writing amid my life as a parent, around soccer practices, hockey games, piano and swim lessons, homework projects, driving duties, cooking, cleaning, washing, folding, and being a great wife I may add! I love my life! I love my children, and my husband, and it's not about this not being enough or being discontent with it. It is about my personal, spiritual journey of forging an innate, undeniable, uncontainable craving to be used by God within the creativity He gave me. Have you ever seen a fruit dehydrator in action? Basically, its purpose is to remove moisture from the fruit, drying it and shrinking it to a leathery state. I fit that shoe, so to speak. I give and give and give, and I don't mind, but I need something of my own to replenish me. As for the leathery state . . . well . . . I'm getting older and I don't like it!

Being a stay-at-home mom has definitely been a tremendous blessing. I was and still am able to be there for my kids day and night when they were little, and pick them up from school today, and be available to them physically and emotionally. But sometimes I wish I had a work place to go to and interact with people with the same interests and go for lunch and share laughter or frustrations. Being at home makes me lonely at times and I have to improvise excitement and fascination.

The other day I was about to use my very complicated top-of-the-line juicer with its intricate pieces that go together in a very modern and gadget-like way. When we first got it, it used to frustrate me with its perplexing parts, but now it doesn't intimidate me anymore. I approach it with confidence, and in my mind I am Angelina Jolie (don't judge me!) in an action-packed movie, strong, capable, endowed with extreme ability at putting a weapon together. I do it with ease and a dexterous, fluid rhythm, approaching an intricate task with strong, tough, yet feminine, and may I add sexy movements. Just trust me: some juicers require a lot of assembly. And so I pout my lips as the gears click, positioning the metal grooves perfectly in sync, then hold them down with one hand, and with the other I slide the mesh screen on top, thrust the pulp discharge over the screen, threading together the gears moving with sleek rotating sounds, and binding the plastic cover tightly into place. I latch the outside arms, fastening them into place, secure the feeding chute, and *boom* turn the button on! Very exhilarating for a housewife with a lot of imagination!

I simply don't want to lose myself in all the years dedicated to parenting and "regular" life, Xeroxing one day into the next, unaware that times move fast and my dreams and aspirations are still on the back burner. The words of famous painter Vincent Van Gogh resonate true, "A great fire burns within me, but no one stops to warm themselves by it, and passers-by only see a wisp of smoke."

And so, the dehydrated fruit syndrome pops up because I give so much of myself to the kids and family every day—to my house duties, to life's many challenges, to our marriage (a great one, but it takes work), to extended family members—yet I deeply feel that God has given me creativity for a reason and He expects me to use it on a daily basis.

Some of you are already using your creative gifts, and perhaps are perfectly happy and fulfilled with purpose and satisfaction. You have found your rhythm and feel confirmed by God in your fulfillment. Every person's journey is different, and every passion has a different definition for each one of us. I believe creativity is part of our finite fiber and being available to its realm can bring us so much joy. And your profession does not have to coincide with your creative passion. For me, aside from writing, baking is a creative outlet. While I bake, I feel a certain surrender of my thoughts and a little bit of my soul . . . Watching chocolate melt in a pot while eggs are frothing thick in a mixing bowl, the fresh awakening of lemon zest filling the air, cinnamon, nutmeg, pumpkin spices blending in a rich lather of cheesecake, the soothing warmth of fresh baked apple pie—all this forms an artistic landscape for my soul, giving me a sense of euphoric joy, belonging to something beautiful, peaceful, and happy.

Many of my friends who are mothers and fathers have other aspirations that ignite their hearts while they attend their daily jobs. One of my girlfriends is a nurse, and she loves her job, but she dreams of opening a bed and breakfast one day; another is to be involved in marine biology, even though he is a blinds installer; another is to be decorator; another is to be an astronaut (she says she has always felt a special connection to the stars). That special connection was put there by God. I am not saying we should all quit our professions, and follow a dream. But what I am saying is despite our daily employment, we are filled with other desires which we can still follow, as a hobby, or as a part-time job, now or later in life.

The very much celebrated poet T. S. Eliot worked as a clerk in the underground basement of a prestigious London bank, crunching numbers daily, but yet, even though successful at his banking career, he had a deep beckoning and yearning to write. God makes us multilateral in our passions. We are all visionaries with hidden ideas and talents. He created us this way because it was more exciting for Him to have His children be artistic, creative, inventive, and passionate. The world is more beautiful with us in it this way.

I feel I can be a better parent to my children if my own individualism doesn't get lost in the shuffle of life. Before I became a wife and mother, I existed as a separate entity filled with my own dreams, desires, and longings. Of course life shifts and takes on different texture, but I want to make sure that from time to time I rehydrate my artistic self and replenish my mind and my individual core. Basically plump the raisin back into a grape!

We all started out with a box of crayons in our hands, and I want to inspire my own children to always challenge and inspire themselves, to be fascinated not only with coloring inside the lines, but most importantly also with coloring outside the lines, for I believe that is the place where imagination, problem solving, and self-discoveries are made.

For me, craving creativity in my life is instinctive and intrinsic. In other words, I just can't help myself. I am always thinking of writing something, of putting different color schemes together, of embellishing my cooking, of pretending to be in an action movie (even though my weapon is a juicer!). It may sound silly, but I promise you, God expects us to be creative, whether we are parents or not.

> For we are God's masterpiece. He has created us anew in Christ Jesus, so we can do the good things he planned for us long ago. (Ephesians 2:10)

Chapter 9

Be Bored and Suffer Well

*Today's students are let down easily by teachers and wrapped
in cotton wool by some parents.*
—Anna Patty, *The Sydney Morning Herald*

A very long while back, my sister-in-law was quietly reading a book
in her bedroom when her two-year-old walked in. She said to her
mom, "Agatha Christie," which was in fact the author of the book her
mom was reading. My sister-in-law was blissfully shocked at her young
daughter's prowess when she distinctly heard her say "Agatha Christie."
She proudly looked at her genius child, imagining her future as a savant
and all the brilliant things she was going to accomplish, when she noticed
her little girl's finger reaching way inside her nose and says it again, "I got
a crusty." So much for all the hopes of being the mother of an exceptional
child— great story for her future wedding though!

Of course, as parents, we hope and desire the absolute best for our
children. And how can we not think this way from the moment we see
their beautiful tiny faces . . . We, too, felt extremely blessed with this
precious, freshly born baby, untamed, not yet molded into anything. We
were actually freaking out by the sense of responsibility to do the very
best for both the kids, feed them the right foods, the best information,
carve their souls, and nourish their minds according to God's will.

The instinct is to want our children to be happy, to experience
laughter, joy, success, basically a constant stream of blessings. Personally,
when I see my kids laugh with wide cheeks framing their faces with pure

bliss, it fills my soul with delirious delight. I simply hope to only see them brimful with happiness, joy, and contentment. I know that can't be possible, so I inevitably see them sad, confused, sorrow emerging beneath their eyes full of tears, suffering from life's unavoidable armfuls of grief. Then, I just want to leap and cup them close, protecting them from anything that may tamper with their happiness.

"I just want you to be happy, honey," my mom would say to me when I was growing up. Our worldly desire is to seek pleasure and avoid pain, but we are not designed that way by our heavenly Father. He wants all to suffer well, so to speak—to grow in our faith, learn from our mistakes, gain wisdom, innovate out of boredom, create amazing things, make a difference in the world, reinvent some more, change others' lives for the better, be supremely happy for a while, have constant peace and joy, then start all over again. Believe me it all sounds very logical, and obviously I understand it, but my barely acquired wisdom goes out the window when faced with everyday ordeals.

Just the other day, my son forgot his school spirit T-shirt at home, and so he called me from school to ask me to bring it to him. He also forgets his lunch at home many times. My daughter forgot her homework one day, and her daily binder another day. What did I do about it, you may wonder? Well, as a parent endowed with extreme discernment, and excellent parental skills, each time, I jumped from my breakfast table, in the middle of my warm soothing oatmeal, ignored God's imaginary pointed finger moving back and forth in disapproval, and drove all the forgotten items to my precious babes. I could see my girl's little heart beating like a hummingbird's in stress and worry, fearing she will get in trouble, and my middle-schooler's brooding face, him being the only one not participating without wearing the required shirt. No, no, I could not let that happen to the apples of my eye. I went ahead and rescued them...

My children were not in a destitute and hopeless situation by any means. They needed no guarding from any evil, but they do need protection from becoming entitled, dependent, unaccountable, fussed-over human beings. This is not just a presupposed story; I really did do the rescuing in a most panicked manner, not realizing that I may fall in the drastic category of either becoming a "helicopter parent" or a "lawn mower" one. The latter is my favorite, which means to mow down any obstacles that may impede a child's happiness and well-being, smoothing over any problems in order to prevent him or her from experiencing pain, disappointment, or frustration.

You may be more familiar with the "helicopter parent," term, which assumes the role of a literal and symbolical hovering over a child's life, trying to control with exigence anything that concerns the child, from scrutinizing their homework, their friends, their habits, to offering excessive advice and suffocating involvement. I, for one, cannot stand having someone hovering over my shoulder. It annoys me, so imagine how our children feel!

I do have to swallow my pride, and humbly admit that I tend to slip in both parenting styles, especially the "lawn mower" one. Naturally as a parent, I want my children to have more opportunities and fewer struggles than I had growing up. Despite the many hardships, my mother had delicious food on the table, clothes on my back, and took me on modest vacations. I did live during a time when I didn't have as many distractions as kids have today. I lived a simple life. Because my mom was a single parent, I had many responsibilities at a young age so I rarely became bored.

My Romanian generation is called the "generation with the key around the neck," which literally means that, as young as elementary age, we all had our house key on a brown twine around our neck, tucked inside our collar. We walked to school together with other kids our age, came home to our conglomerated apartments, took the key out, and while still hanging around our neck, we leaned forward to reach the key lock and hear it open. I would walk in and find my thermos full of soup with a piece of bread beside it, left there by my mother before she went to work early that morning.

I had no television to entertain me while I ate my food; I was to do my homework, tidy up my room, and not open the door to anyone I didn't know. Until my mother got home, the next-door neighbor kept an eye on me. If I forgot something at home, my mom was definitely not able or willing to rescue me in any way. *I learned not to forget and not to depend on my mother remembering.* I had to find a way to become more responsible and more organized. If I forgot my lunch . . . well, I had to depend on the kindness of my friends!

I also realized that the antidote to boredom was my imagination. I developed an essential and early ability to preoccupy myself either by reading, writing, coloring, painting, creating something, inventing, sewing clothes for my dolls, running outside and playing with my friends who were in the same boat as I. If I scraped my knees, I learned to get up and keep playing. It's just the way it was then. Different times, different culture perhaps.

For some strange unknown reason there has been a shift in parenting in our today's culture. We have travelled from simple to overly complicated, and a lot of parents (me included) overprotect their children and try their best to make them happy. We end up treating them like fragile creatures, about to break if they suffer a little, and we end up, as my pastor Craig Groeschel says, bowing "at the altar of their happiness." He says in a sermon that "we give our children praise they don't deserve, give them things they didn't earn, give them freedom they can't handle, thus we risk too little, rescue them too quickly, and reward too frequently . . . we need to worry less about today's happiness and more about tomorrow's readiness."

I definitely rescue too quickly and at times give both the children things they didn't earn. Of course kids don't constantly need to earn everything they have, but if there is something specific that they desire, working for it teaches them responsibility, accountability, appreciation, and respect. Lately our soon-to-be teenage son wants to have more and more freedom, such as being able to stay up later, increased sleepovers, unsupervised time with his friends at the movie theatre, to be trusted with hanging out at the mall with a best friend, etc. So, we make him earn the right to these privileges, by completing his chores on a daily basis, maintaining good grades, speaking respectfully to us, showing awareness of others' needs in our house by volunteering "unappointed" tasks. We want him to understand that his desired freedom is not an automatic merit or endowment.

Trying to protect my children from experiencing disappointment and struggles, only teaches them to be completely dependent on others for their happiness (i.e., ME—the mother), and thus resent when no one is helping them out. I learned that the hard way, by running to school to provide them with their forgotten homework; the more I did it, the more they forgot it! The kids counted on me to bail them out because the fault always fell on the momma: "I wouldn't have gotten a bad grade if you just brought my paper to school," or "I got sick because I didn't have my jacket." I was creating spoiled kids, with a touch of entitlement. I love my children to a fault, but I had to stop running to their aid—smoothing things over, and preventing them from experiencing the discomforts of real life. I believe we are expected to suffer in life. God never promised us constant happiness; we will face many trials and tribulations which teach us to reach out to Him more and more. Learning to suffer "well" early in life, will teach our children required endurance, which empowers them with solution-finding skills and learning valuable lessons, and also developing a Christlike character.

It is okay to fall, scrape your knees, and then learn to get back up. I watched a friend of mine choosing not to rescue her six-year-old daughter when she was afraid at the shoreline of the beach due to a school of little fish: "Mom! Come get me! I'm afraid of the fish!" I was just about to leap forward to scoop her up, when her mother said: "Don't be afraid. You can get out by yourself. Just be careful to go around them. I am watching you, honey." She was so excited to run into her mother's loving arms: "I did it all by myself!"

"I am so proud of you!" her mother responded beaming with pride.

I, too, learned that day. I would have shot out of my comfy beach chair in a panic, picked my daughter, as she continued to cry on her towel soaking up all my coddling, "Mommy made it all better, didn't she, baby girl?" #lawnmower mother. As parents, we are here to help navigate, not accommodate at all costs.

When my children walk around the house moaning: "I am sooo bored," it drives me crazy. I tell them to go read, help me cook, play with your sibling (which actually means drive each other crazy), fix something that's broken, play outside! Of course all of these suggestions are met with "ughh" noises.

I saw this acronym for the word "BORED" on Facebook, so I pinned it on my fridge, so when the kids start whining again I point to it. Have you:

Been creative?

Outside play?

Read a book?

Exercised twenty minutes?

Done something helpful?

Too much of the same thing can be very boring especially if it's a brainless screen-watching activity. What happened to good old imagination, and forcing the brain to shoot excited neurons, awakening frustrated little minds? Come to think of it I am not entirely sure my children even know how to climb a tree . . . Hmm . . . I will test them on that very soon!

I took a careful step back from becoming a "helicopter" or a "lawnmower" parent. Aside from the fact that these labels sound kind of creepy, I really don't want to be annoying, or coddle my children, and condition them to expect indulgence from us the parents. We are not here to ensure their happiness or void their lives of any discomfort, but equip them with God's help to experience joy during good and bad times alike, and perhaps also remind ourselves of the same truth.

Chapter 10

Discipline, Schmicipline

"Oh sweet, powerful Lord, I thank You for the gift of my children . . . I love them with all my heart and I am humbled that You trust me with the job of teaching them to grow into mature, wise adults who love You passionately. But oh dear Lord, please help me not to take one of those particular 'gifts' and put it back in that precious gift box . . . I fear for his safety today, so protect him, Lord, by zipping his sweet, precious little lips. Help me to show Your love, patience, and mercy through gritted teeth. Hallelujah, it is finished. Pass the ibuprofen. Amen!"

—Cari Garrett, mother

It is Mother's Day morning and we are getting ready to go to church. I can sleep in this day (as part of my gift), but wake up early anyway (out of habit), prop my pillow against the headboard, and chuckle to myself as I hear shuffles of feet, plates clonking in the kitchen, shushing, and "stop it, you two!" warnings outside my bedroom door.

"Be happy, and make Mom's day special," my husband further nudges the kids. I have a tiny buzz in my belly, anticipating being celebrated. Yay!

Breakfast in bed is beautifully served, but I can tell on my children's pouting faces that they have been in trouble already (possibly arguing over who did more to prepare my meal, and who did a better job picking out flowers from our little garden). Whatever . . . It is going to be a great day. It is *my* day after all, when everyone *has* to be on their best behavior or else! What can go wrong?

As I get dressed, I hear a notch of increased agitation in my husband's attempt to caution our eight-year-old girl and twelve-year-old son not to fight, bicker, push, shove, argue, or create any commotion to upset Mom today. The son apparently can't help be provocative and an instigator, demanding fairness in every situation. He is on the threshold of adolescence, full of fluctuating hormones, monumental increases in testosterone levels, and mood swings that oscillate from instantly angry and annoyed to extremely excited and bouncing off the walls.

At the same time, the eight-year-old takes full advantage of her brother's emotional "ticking bomb" syndrome, and carefully exploits her birth order, competently dishing out blame and responsibility on her older sibling.

I am in the bathroom, when I hear them fighting in the living room.

"He took my hair elastics!"

"No I didn't. You're lying! I was just playing with them."

"No you weren't. You wanted to shoot them across the room!"

"What did I say to both of you just a few minutes ago? It's Mother's Day. Stop fighting for once!" my husband interjects with frustration.

There is no way I am leaving my secure, free-of-stress bathroom, and emerge on the battle field on *my* day. I take a deep breath, and finish putting on my makeup. I am finally ready to go, when both the kids are bickering over a 99-cents pack of candy.

"This is mine. You ate yours already. I saw you," his sister says as she grabs the candy out of his hands.

"Yeah, but I shared with you, so now you owe me some of yours," he responds.

"You opened it!!!???" she yells in shock, as tears of despair roll down her face.

"She's just happy to get me in trouble. This is all her fault!"

I am disappointed and angry at how petty and selfish they both are on so many levels right now! Fueled by their self-absorbed attitudes, and by my elevated Mother's Day expectations, I announce that they are both punished. They are not to have any dessert (when, or *if*, we go out to a restaurant, 'cause I may not feel like going anymore), any treats, sugar, or any access to their electronic devices, including television, for the rest of the day. Their father backs me up and we are both called "mean" and "unfair."

This is supposed to be a day when I can do no wrong, when I am celebrated for working hard, kissing boo-boos, checking foreheads with high fever, cleaning spills and throw-up, cooking, cleaning, helping with homework projects, being a taxi driver for all activities, being—what I think—a pretty good mom! Good grief, I spend my days hoping that I am a good parent, a godly role model, trying to teach them good manners and values, and then at night, after they fall asleep I cry through my prayers, thinking I could have shown more patience, more wisdom . . .

The kids just don't get it. I am not their enemy. We, the parents, are not the enemy. We are their biggest fans! But I find myself in the courtroom every day listening to complaints from both the children— usually my son litigating his own case, the constant victim of unfair, unjust accusations and treatments from his sister, or being frustrated by our parental enforcements.

"Why can't I watch this movie?"

"Because it's PG-13."

"But it's only rated PG13 for violence and some language."

"Ha! '*some* language'!?"

"Please, this is so unfair. All my other friends have watched it."

"Sorry, son. 'No' is a complete sentence."

Motion denied.

OR

"But this is a Disney show, Mom. A lot of my friends are watching it."

"I know, but you are a little girl with an innocent mind, and this is not a show where they speak respectfully to their parents."

OR

"Mom, I know you said we are punished from TV all day, but we have been getting along so far. . ." (His sister is peeking from around the corner as her brother asks me for grace.) "Can we please watch just one episode of something?" (He is trying to renegotiate my original verdict.)

"No, honey." I am sure that my kids actually see me with a big "NO" plastered on my forehead. "I am however, very grateful that you two are getting along. That's the way it should be. Thank you."

"This is so unfair. Just half an hour of TV . . . Please? We won't fight, or argue or drive you crazy anymore."

I can't help but smile at his ardent plea, but the defendants have many prior convictions of the same nature, so I have to be a tough parent.

"Nope. You both have to learn that your behavior choices have consequences, and unfortunately you will have to suffer through them." Motion for appeal is denied.

God expects us to discipline our children even when we don't feel like it, even on Mother's Day . . . It would have been much easier and convenient for me to ignore their mean spirits for the sake of having a good day. And maybe I should have. I don't ever know with certainty that what I am doing is the right thing, because parenting is hard. It is for me, anyway. Maybe I am not used to sibling rivalry, being the only child, so the perpetual probing, prodding, irritating, smirking, annoying smiles, instigative responses are just "healthy" dynamics that I don't understand. My husband grew up with four other siblings, so while I spend most of my days hyperventilating, with arms akimbo, and a warning pointed finger, he is more relaxed, sometimes unaware of all the noise and conflict.

Maybe some of you are reading this and laughing out loud at my fretting and frustration: "Relax, lady, kids will be kids. They will fight, bicker, and rough-house. It's how brothers and sisters form bonds for life." And maybe you are right, for on the rare occasion I do see them curled up on the couch together, after all the wrangle and frolic, sharing a space, with rosy cheeks and tousled hair, finally relenting into their childhood innocence and love for each other. The point is that nobody said that having children will be an easy task, and I am grateful that God knew that, so He gave us so many verses in the Bible pertaining to discipline, to help and assist us in being good parents to these blessed creatures He bestowed on us.

I still remember my mom punishing me for one week during my summer vacation. I called her a "cow," when she wouldn't let me go to an overnight party with my teen friends. I am not proud of it, but I was a teenager expecting my freedom to be granted whenever I asked for it. In retrospect, of course, I thank my mom for keeping me home away from lustful temptations, peer pressure, and who knows what other ungodly activities. I know, our time is coming fairly soon when the teen arena will unleash upon us with all its challenges, and then I will call some of *you* for guidance!

Tough love is meant to be tough. When our kids were little, we stayed home from birthday parties they were looking forward to, because of temper tantrums. Now they may stay home from desired get-togethers with friends, because of disrespectful behavior or insolent attitudes. Do I feel bad? Yes. I sometimes question, and second-guess my parenting choices, but I pray and hope that I am doing what is best for the character of my children.

I have compiled most of the discipline verses from the Bible on a large piece of white paper and hang it on our fridge for my husband and I to refer to it as a constant guide, and for our children to refer to anytime they have a problem with our rules and regulations. I want our kids to realize that discipline is not intended as a way for parents to be mean, unfair, cruel, or authoritative with no good valid reason.

God disciplines all of us including the adults, because He loves us. So, we discipline our children out of love, to nurture them, educate, guide, and prepare them to be, as my church says, fully devoted followers of Christ. So on the days parenting feels like an inconvenience, or like a tiring thankless, relentless job, here is all the advice from the Word of God, and what meets our eyes every time we open our fridge. (Which is a lot!)

1. "To learn, you must love discipline. It is stupid to hate correction" (Proverbs 12:1).
2. "A wise child accepts a parent's discipline. A young mocker refuses to listen" (Proverbs 13:1).
3. "If you refuse to discipline your children, it proves you don't love them. But if you love your children, you will be quick to discipline them" (Proverbs 13:24).
4. "Discipline your children, and they will give you happiness and peace of mind" (Proverbs 29:17).
5. "Fathers, don't aggravate your children. If you do, they will become discouraged and quit trying" (Colossians 3:21).

6. "My child, don't ignore it when the Lord disciplines you and don't be discouraged when he corrects you. For the Lord disciplines those he loves . . ." (Hebrews 12:5–6).
7. "And now a word to your fathers. Don't make your children angry by the way you treat them. Rather bring them up with discipline and instruction approved by the Lord" (Ephesians 6:4).
8. "No discipline is enjoyable while it is happening—it is painful! But afterward there will be a quiet harvest of right living for those who are trained in this way" (Hebrews 12:11).
9. "Children, obey your parents because you belong to the Lord, for this is the right thing to do" (Ephesians 6:1).
10. "But you must remain faithful to the things you have been taught. You know they are true, for you know you can trust those who taught you. You have been taught the Holy Scriptures from childhood, and they have given you the wisdom to receive the salvation that comes by trusting in Christ Jesus" (2 Timothy 3:14–15).
11. "'Honor your father and mother.'" This is the first of the Ten Commandments that ends with a promise. And this is the promise: If you honor your father and mother, 'things will go well for you and you will live a long life, full of blessings'" (Ephesians 6:1–3).

Number eleven is my favorite because after all, we sure want all this for our children, don't we?

Chapter 11

Bring Up an Altruist

We make a living by what we get. We make a life by what we give.
—Winston Churchill

My mother is a giver. It is simply built in her nature, I guess, or maybe because she grew up very poor in a tiny village in northern Romania, and thus it has taught her humility and giving to others. Either way, she loves to give. As a child, I recall that each time my mom cooked anything she would first ask me to take a pot of food to the neighbor, "Take this to Mrs. Melania," or to different neighbors on different occasions. I didn't question her; it's just the way she did things, almost as if she gave her first to Christ in everything. Her philosophy was that sharing and giving makes one content and happy inside. She was always excited to bless others. In return, the pot of food given away was always returned full. The mere purpose of this blue, chipped, enamel vessel was to deliver goodness back and forth. What a lucky pot!

One thing I observed in my life is that the ones that have little give the most to one another. Why is that? I, too, wanted to start the trend of a blue pot of my own with the neighbors, but they seemed taken aback by my zeal and it didn't catch on. Maybe they thought I was crazy, or maybe I live in the wrong neighborhood, maybe they don't need my food, or maybe it is just a simple cultural difference. I just wanted to flex my altruistic muscle. You may wonder what does *altruistic* mean, so according to *The Oxford College Dictionary*, it is "the belief or practice of selfless concern for the well-being of others."

Jesus may be the ultimate altruist, who self-sacrificed for our benefit, so naturally I would like to see my two children understand that having is really in the giving. *Good luck with that, Roxana.* Our society now is built more on accumulation of earthly possessions, living in affluent neighborhoods, and getting more "stuff." The younger generation is inclined toward hedonistic attitudes, as pleasure is their proper aim in life. Think how easily children are concerned with the word *mine*: "That's mine! Give it back!" "my toy," "my space," "my snack," etc. My own two kids don't wake up every morning saying, "Mom, Dad, what can I do for you today?" (HA-HA). We are not born givers, but takers of food, attention, love, and time; therefore, it is hard to bring up children as selfless human beings. And when exactly can I fit in altruism when our lives are filled with homework, soccer, piano, gymnastics, swimming, play dates, church, vacations, and family time?! Most of what I hear parents around me say is, "We are so busy all the time," or "We have so much going on. It's overwhelming!"

Apparently, though, God expects us to be consumed with generosity, "You will be enriched in every way so that you can always be generous. And when we take your gifts to those who need them, they will thank God" (2 Corinthians 9:11).

When I tell my children that "having is in the giving," they look at me perplexed, as if I am crazy! To a child, having is in the "having," not in the giving. It takes determination, diligence, and discipline to teach them a generous spirit. The easiest way is for them to see us, the parents, be zealous givers and helpers—with our material resources, but also with our time, prayer, and emotional outreach. I have to admit I am not a forerunner in this area, but many of my friends are, and I am learning a lot from them. My friend, Rachelle, a mother of five, is one of the most altruistic people I know. She started a program called "Helping Hands. A Ministry of Hope." She helps needy moms with their nurseries by sewing linens, painting walls, and babysits for free. She is consumed by outreach no matter where she goes. Her children, no doubt, are learning from her selfless role-modeling. Another mom I know started RAOK—Random Acts of Kindness with her children. She not only sacrificially adopted a little girl from Ethiopia, but is also deeply involved with Jonah's Journey, providing care for children of incarcerated mothers. Through RAOK, she involves her children in taking the focus completely off of themselves and onto others. They literally find a need and fill it. Her third grader helps neighbors by bringing in their garbage cans, or they help the elderly with their groceries. In many ways they become hyper aware of others, and how they can be a blessing to them.

Prompted by these mothers' charitable example, I also tried to follow in their footsteps and involved my children in many giving opportunities. My son started tutoring younger, underprivileged kids at a local center. During different holidays we make cards for the nursing home. They each have to make one hundred cards. My daughter creates elaborate handmade cards, while my minimalist son creates one card on his computer and then presses Print for ninety-nine more!

Around Thanksgiving and Christmas, there are soup kitchens where our family can go and serve the homeless dinner. Also, every year both the kids participate in the Samaritan's Purse collection, through which they fill a shoe box with presents for the impoverished children around the world (Operation Christmas Child). One year, we even received a thank-you note from a four-year-old that lives in Zambia, which further impressed on the kids to get involved in the Compassion International program and sponsor a little girl from India.

I believe that giving is free. All that it costs us is the condition of our heart. If we give with prying fingers, the giving feels like a burden, with the price of regret attached to it, but if we are freely generous, excited to bless others, our giving then becomes free and our hearts and lives overflow with joy and contentment. My pastor says that we are the most like our Lord and Savior when we are giving and forgiving.

I pray that generosity will become second nature to my two children. Dave Ramsey says that, "Giving is precious to watch when the kids are young, and fulfilling to watch as they grow into adulthood. Giving makes them less self-centered . . . and brings your kids depth of character. Those who never give become shallow, self-centered, and miserable adults. Givers are better spouses, better employees, better people."[4]

The other day I saw a really cool T-shirt in my daughter's closet. When I asked her where she got it from she said, "I got it from church, because

I was the only one that tithed every Sunday, so they gave me a shirt as a gift." First of all, I had no idea that my daughter was faithfully tithing at eight years old. She earns money through chores, and lemonade stands. I am ashamed to admit it, but I have not impressed on her the importance of tithing as much as I should. In fact, I have to humbly confess that it took me a long time to joyfully give ten percent of our income away to God. Whenever we made less it was easier, but when we earned more it became harder to be generous . . . God says, "Test me in this," says the LORD Almighty, "and see if I will not throw open the floodgates of heaven and pour out so much blessing that there will not be room enough to store it" (Malachi 3:10 NIV).

So then every time I tithed, I was waiting to see what God would do for me, like a genie in a bottle. It took me some time to fully comprehend how giving to God and others is a blessing to me, to my family. My husband was very patient with my spoiled attitude, as he is a very joyful giver, helper, and servant of God.

I tell my kids they should be generous every day in some way, wherever they are. They can offer help to a teacher, show appreciation through their actions, hug a friend who is sad, tie shoelaces for a kindergartner, open the door for an elder, etc. I explain to them that God cares about what happens in their lives, and He pour blessings on them through friendships, by giving them health, happy opportunities, and peace at school. Life will feel like it is filled with little miracles, no matter where they go or what they do.

My daughter lost her iPod this past summer by mistake (and we all know that means she lost the extension of her hand!), so at Christmas her brother spent forty dollars of his own money and bought her a new (used) one. The look on her surprised, but excited face made his sacrificial giving worth it, and also deepened their sibling relationship. Because of this, she followed his example and gave back to him as well. That is all God's doing in their young hearts. Is it a rare occurrence? YES! You must know by my previous chapters how hectic life is at our house, but the seed of generosity has been planted.

This past year I read a story about a very kind ten-year-old-girl, who has decided to raise money for our brave soldiers abroad by auctioning her brand-new American Girl doll. She simply thought it was more important to help those who miss their homes and families. She raised $1,560 and used it to make care packages for those who serve our country.

Zachary Bonner, at seven years of age, started the Little Red Wagon Foundation to help homeless children in our country. Hannah Taylor, at the tender age of five, started The Ladybug Foundation to also help the homeless and raised over two million dollars. Now, a teenager, she speaks passionately about her cause to many schools around the country. Craig, age twelve, and his brother Mark Kielburger created Free the Children organization concerned with changing child labor laws overseas. There are many others like these altruistic children, whose hearts are moved and burdened with other people's plights and needs. God must fill the heavens with laughter of delight seeing His little ones do His mighty will: "Don't let anyone think less of you because you are young. Be an example to all believers in what you say, in the way you live, in your love, your faith, and your purity" (1 Timothy 4:12).

I would have to assume that Blake Mycoskie, the founder of TOMS, must have been a big-hearted kid. He is changing the lives and well-being of many people by providing shoes, safe drinking water, and eye wear through his philanthropic ventures. Many of us wear TOMS shoes and we are helping a human being in a different part of the world have shoes also. By the way, TOMS stands for people having a better TOMorrow. (I always thought Tom was his name!)

Another outstanding person that caught my interest is Benjamin Olewine III, who helped a random waitress by paying her way through nursing school in Harrisburg, Pennsylvania. He is also a charitable person in many other ways, but how rare and beautiful his gesture was. It moved me to tears. Yes, he has the financial freedom to do this but he is aware of God's expectations: "When someone has been given much, much will be required in return" (Luke 12:48).

I desperately want my kids to experience the incomparable excitement, giddiness, and joy that come with making someone's life better. It is quite euphoric, and it releases for the moment an emotion of complete peace, and true love. Then, you'll have to do it over and over again to recapture that fantastic exalted feeling.

I remember one year ago when our family met Mrs. Pauline at a nearby nursing home. The kids, of course, shuffled their feet but I nudged them along to go in every room and offer to pray with the elderly. Mrs. Pauline was sitting in front of a small TV watching classic movies, and finishing her Jell-O cup. She was so excited to see her small room filled with people, but most of all she loved our children. They prayed for her, taking turns reading from the Bible, as she had her eyes closed taking its truth in by murmuring, "Yes, Lord. Yes, Lord." (I did have to stop my son from reading Psalm 23:4—"Even though I walk through the valley of the shadow of death . . ." Can you imagine?! *Hi, Mrs. Pauline. You are old, and this verse seems appropriate.*) We hugged her and she said that no one comes to visit her anymore, as some of her relatives have passed away, and some lived too far. I could tell she was sad to see us leave, but we promised to come back on her birthday. A couple of months later she met Jesus due to her illness. My kids were very sad and felt prompted to go back to the nursing home and visit more people. We did, and we even sang to a beautiful old lady who was passing on before our eyes. At first I wanted to shield my kids from witnessing death, but my daughter held the lady's hand as my son prayed for her (yes, Psalm 23:4 this time), and she closed her bright blue eyes shut. There was no one else in the room but us and the nurse. We wept. The children then realized that she would have died all alone if they weren't there that day.

Giving sacrificially for the benefit of others is all that altruism is about. Spending time when others need you, despite your busy schedule, buying groceries for a needy family, regardless of your tight budget, are all ways of making God smile and He will bless you for it when you least expect it. Bringing up altruistic children can only result in benevolent adults. Some of us may not have endless financial resources to bless others continually, but we all have *time* to give away, even if it's a little bit of it. Altruism comes in different forms. It can make the biggest difference, and I want my son and my daughter to understand that it pleases God when we bless each other with the most precious currency of all: LOVE.

Chapter 12

Love Those Enemies!

But I will not dwell too much on what knocked me down, because what knocked me down is not as important as what made me stand up.
—Aija Mayrock, *The Survival Guide to Bullying*

If you are an avid watcher of Christmas movies, then you probably will be familiar with the movie *A Christmas Story*, in which, among other things, Ralphie gets bullied by the yellow-eyed kid: Scut Farkus. It seems the bullying goes on every day, consisting of verbal condescension, physical intimidation, and provocation. With a feeling of inferiority and fear, Ralphie and his friends succumb to their tormentor until one day Ralphie snaps under pressure and physically fights back, with punching fists, and a litany of verbal irreverence, leaving Scut Farkus with a bleeding nose, and wallowing in defeated sobs and tears. I don't know about you, but I cheer for Ralphie at that retaliative moment, even commending him for finally taking a stand and teaching that bully a lesson. It feels so good to finally see the persecutor evicted from the bullying arena, but the Bible instructs us very differently when it comes to our day-to-day enemies: "But I say, don't resist an evil person. If someone slaps you on the right cheek, offer the other cheek also. . . . But I say, love your enemies! Pray for those who persecute you!" (Matthew 5:39, 44).

"Love your neighbor as yourself," instructs Mark 12:31. Then you know what . . . I must practice a lot of self-loathing! "She didn't just write this!" you say in shocking disbelief, but here is my salute to *#transparency*. It is very hard to love some people, especially when our fifteen-month-old daughter was in a hospital fighting for her little life with a bone infection and your husband's employer is not allowing him to take off to the hospital saying: "Yeah, sorry your daughter is sick and all but I need my house to be finished first." Or when your neighbor calls the police because a plastic arrow landed in her yard one time in the ten years of living next to her, and no matter how hard you try she just chooses to be mean, unkind, and harsh to you and your kids. Or when a friend lies about you behind your back, hurting you to the core with betrayal.

The last thing on my mind in all of these and many other circumstances was to love these hostile people, or pray for them, or have a compassionate heart filled with wisdom and forgiveness. No way! I saw red with anger, and desired to retaliate as soon as possible. How can God expect me, as a bona fide sinner, to outpour love when I am brimful with detest? I find it close to physically impossible to actually bow my head in prayer for these people. My words lock up in my throat, strained by justified unwillingness, as a very difficult surrender to God's will finally escapes: "Dear God, I don't feel like praying for those who persecute me . . . Please forgive me for my reluctant heart, but my will to please You is higher than my will to feel entitled in my loathness. I know these feelings are not from You, God, so I pray You give me the strength to be forgiving. Amen." For now, that's all I can emotionally afford.

> "Pray for those who persecute you. In that way, you will be acting as true children of your Father in heaven. For he gives sunlight to both the evil and the good. . . . If you love only those who love you, what reward is there for that? . . . If you are kind only to your friends, how are you different from anyone else?" (Matthew 5:44–47)

This all makes logical sense in every way, I just need it explained to my heart . . . I want so much for my own two children to fully grasp this amazing wisdom that will enable them to lead a life of joy, and experience emotional peace. But how can I embed this profoundly wise biblical directive into their young minds? It is hard for me at my age to remember and apply these instructions.

Last month, my oldest came home from school and told me he was not welcomed by another boy to join in a specific game they were playing. My son asked if he could play and this boy said curtly: "No! Now, go away." Seconds later, when another classmate asked the same question as my son, the answer was "Yes," and with a cliquish look, followed by a shared smirk, the group of boys ignored my kid. He was sad for the rest of the day. He felt excluded and unwanted. Was this an example of bullying? I think so. The *Oxford College Dictionary* defines a bully as "a person who uses strength or powers to harm or intimidate those who are weaker," thus Scut Farkus from the Christmas movie. This definition pertains to the conventional bullying, with physical pushing, and hitting. But bullying can also be verbal like calling someone inappropriate names such as "stupid," "ugly," "fat," etc., using demeaning intimidation, and last but not least, bullying can be done in a social manner. This occurs through ruthless gossiping, outward lies, ignoring, avoiding, and excluding others on purpose. I believe my son was socially bullied. Through the ever-growing social networking, our kids can be cyberbullied via Facebook, group messaging, Instagram, Twitter, and many others I am probably not aware of because I can't keep up with the pace of all of it. This is probably the "easiest" and most "comfortable" form of bullying because it requires no face-to-face confrontation or accountability and is often times anonymous.

Bullying is an increasingly persistent occurrence in our society, taking many forms as I just mentioned, so as a Christian parent how should I explain to my children the biblical advice to "love your enemies," "turn the other cheek," or "not to resist an evil person"? God knew we would all have an extremely challenging time loving one another, for He made it the second most important commandment after first loving Him (Mark 12:30–31).

But when our kids are bullied and hurting, they don't have the mental and emotional energy to assimilate these Bible verses. They just want their pain to stop, and for others to be kind or nice to them. Don't we all? I decided to explore Matthew 5:39, 44–47, and plan an anti-bullying Bible study at our house. I felt that my kids needed to be fully equipped for any bullying that may or may not occur, and learn to respond to it from a Christian perspective. If this is something you also believe necessary, read on to find out how this Bible study with my kids was approached, and how they responded to it.

First of all, bullying happens many times in the Bible, starting with Genesis 27:41: "Esau hated Jacob because he had stolen his blessing." If we further explore this situation, we find out that Jacob manipulated his brother, Esau, in giving up his birthright over a bowl of stew! It sounds pretty silly, but some people are very good at lying, cheating, and taking advantage of the innocent, thus Esau fell prey to premeditated, skillful persecution, and gave up his rightful inheritance to his brother, and it took a very long time for him to forgive Jacob. And then there is Genesis 37:4 which explains the malicious envy of Joseph by all his other brothers: "But his brothers hated Joseph because their father loved him more than the rest of then. They couldn't say a kind word to him." His brothers had consciously decided to hate and begrudge Joseph, out of jealousy and envy. I clarified to my kids that God does not approve of bullying: "Those who intimidate and harass will be gone . . ." (Isaiah 29:20), and that He expects us to take the posture of gentle heartedness, forgiveness, and no retaliation. This is hard to do when we are generally reactive people, and it's even harder to explain to a child the verse in Luke 6:29: "If someone slaps you on one check, offer the other cheek also." Doing so looks like an act of weakness, as if we all should bow down to a bully, and have no choice but to suffer in humiliation and shame.

So, what did Jesus exactly mean by "offering the other cheek"? After staring at this verse for years, finally some adult wisdom slipped into my grown-up brain. When we encounter our harassers, I think that Jesus means we need to present them with an element of surprise. He or she will likely expect us to cower down, tremble in fear, or cry with discouragement and ridicule. Instead we "offer the other cheek" as an unexpected solution, declaring to the bullies that their insults are not going to affect us negatively. Turning the other cheek, translates into composure, controlled emotion, calmness, and even patience amid the situation. When Jesus instructs us to "not resist an evil person" in Matthew 5:39, I think He means not to take revenge or get angry in return. We need to stay calm, collected, and not say ungodly things that we would later regret.

We all have the right, including our children, to feel righteous anger toward someone that is cruel and mean, but we should not let our anger consume us from the inside out. Jesus also showed righteous anger at the Pharisees for their hypocrisy in Matthew 23, and Matthew 21:12 where He cleared the holy temple of all the merchants, knocking over tables, being angry at the people who had defiled the place of prayer. In Mark 3:2, Jesus' "enemies watched him closely" to see if He would heal on the Sabbath. Jesus "looked around at them angrily because he was deeply saddened by their hard hearts" (verse 5). Jesus got angry at His enemies because He loved them and was saddened by their ungodly attitude. Ephesians 4:26 says, "And don't sin by letting anger control you." None of us can really avoid anger completely, but we must learn to respond in it with wisdom, and hopefully teach our children the same wisdom with God's help. Fueled anger can escalate into hatred, and desire for revenge which doesn't do anyone any good. That's why God directs us, as hard as it may be, to love our enemy and to pray for those who persecute us (Matthew 5:44–47).

My son asked, "How can I 'love' my enemy, when I don't really feel like it?" Well, isn't that the question of the day . . . "I don't feel like it either," I explained to him, "but Jesus wants to chisel at our hardened hearts, by practicing compassion and understanding." This is very hard to do because it goes against our sinful nature, so the younger we are guided into practicing God's wisdom on this the better it will be.

Because bullying is such a serious concern in our children's lives, despite how old they may be, I decided to write a preparatory Bible study, gathering many Bible verses that will help my kids, and perhaps yours, with presupposed bullying situations. You may think me crazy for writing all this out, but when you have kids you must do extreme stuff. So, here are my words to my children:

- A person may bully to gain power over others by hurting them, to become popular, to intimidate for fun, to impress others around them, or because bullying is how they get self-importance. Maybe bullying is all they know how to be . . . At times, a bully has a home life that is dysfunctional, with parents that fight, and even physically hurt each other or their children. So, then, a bully hurts others to make himself, or herself, feel better. Trying to think from their point of view makes it easier for us to show compassion and to pray for them. When we do as God says, and "pray for those who persecute us," we achieve two things: we literally pray that the harasser's life changes for the good; and also through prayer we learn not to be bitter or hateful. If you are bullied at school, try not to get scared, or get angry, because that is what a bully expects and wants of you. He or she will gain power from your reaction. Remember Joshua 1:9, "Do not be afraid or discouraged, for the LORD your God is with you wherever you go."

- Stay calm. Look at the person who's trying to harm you and say "STOP" in a calm but firm way: "A fool is quick tempered, but a wise person stays calm when insulted" (Proverbs 12:16).
- Use humor, to change the bully's negative intentions: "A gentle answer deflects anger, but harsh words make tempers flare." For instance, my son was told by a mean boy that he looked really ugly in his yearbook picture. He came home really hurt, so I told him the next time this happens, say this: "I know, right!? I love it! I look so silly!" Also, if someone calls you fat, you can say: "Thank you. I love my food!")
- Do not feel ashamed. You did nothing wrong. Stand up for yourself without using swear words. You can simply say: "I don't care about what you think," and walk away: "Beginning a quarrel is like opening a floodgate, so drop the matter before a dispute breaks out" (Proverbs 17:14).
- Do not take revenge: "Never pay back evil with more evil" (Romans 12:17).
- Avoid being around bullies if possible, even if it takes longer to get to where you need to be, even if you are late for class. I would rather you be safe than on time: "A prudent person foresees danger and takes precautions" (Proverbs 22:3).
- If you see others get bullied, go help them out of their situation safely.
- It goes without saying: "Do not be a bully."
- Tell us, the parents, immediately about any bullying situation. It is extremely important that parents and teachers are aware of any abusive behavior so they can deal with the bully properly. Do not be afraid to

tell grown-ups about this. Telling someone is not tattling at all. There is a huge difference. *Tattling is done for the sake of getting someone in trouble, whereas telling is honestly reaching out for help.* That is why you have parents so we can help you and guide you in any situation.

It is important that the lines of communication are open between our kids and us the parents. I am sure I drive them crazy with all the questions about their daily lives, "What happened at school today?" "Who did you have lunch with?" "What did you and your friends talk about?" "Was anyone mean to you today?" "Were you nice to your friends as well?"

Of course, I don't really get detailed answers—most of the time, depending on their mood they will share more or just simply shrug their shoulders and give me intriguing monosyllables: "yes," "no," "sometimes." Hey, I'll take whatever as long as they know I am interested in their lives. The last thing I want is for them to hide a struggle or an issue they may have.

My daughter is younger so she pours out about her day a little easier than her brother who is a teen soon. But whatever the case, I want our sharing and our communication to feel habitual, typical, instinctive, and an effortless routine. As parents, we want exactly that from our kids, because it promotes confidence, good self-esteem, and solutions to their problems. Bullies are less likely to approach self-assured, positive, confident children.

I hear many stories about how bullying can lead to detrimental issues in our children, like depression, panic attacks, eating disorders, anxiety, and at times even suicide. That's why it is so important to tackle this issue early in our children's lives! Coercion doesn't happen only on the playground anymore. Tormenting others is a pastime for some, especially through social media nowadays.

This chapter is by no means an easy fix for bullying: "A few Bible verses here and there, and *voilà*, no more bullies!" There are times when the authorities—whether school officials or even the police—need to be notified to prevent further harm. Please see the list of sources and help at the end of this chapter for further information.

In the end, God is the One in control over our daily lives, even when our children may be persecuted and dragooned by mean boys and girls. There is always a solution through prayer, patience, and surrendering our problems at God's feet. God also gives us discernment when we need to get involved.

We tell our kids, that we do all that *we* can do, and then let God come through for us, as He always does.

Sources for dealing with bullying:
www.stopbullying.com
www.thebullyproject.com
The movie *An American Girl: Chrissa Stands Strong*
Kids Help Phone: 1-800-668-6868 (more info at www.kidshelpphone.ca)

Chapter 13

Demented Love

"Take your son, your only son—yes Isaac, whom you love so much. . . .
Go and sacrifice him as a burnt offering on one of the mountains,
which I will show you." (Genesis 22:2)

This is what God told Abraham to do with his beloved son Isaac. I often ask myself how willing would I be to offer my own children as a sacrifice for God . . . Would I be able to go through with such a burdening, heartbreaking request out of obedience to Him? I would like to say I would pass God's test, and I secretly hope God will never ask of me such hardship.

The thing is, I am crazy in love with my children, as I am sure you are too. I call it demented love, because it's irrational at times, and there is nothing I wouldn't do for them. As mentioned earlier, our youngest child was sick with a bone infection when she was sixteen months old. I remember looking at her delicate body, her feminine features, and her downy light brown hair with blond fuzz at its ends. Her slender, petite arms laid there full of fever, her little fingers holding on to mine. The sun rays were seeping through the hospital window, giving her a heavenly glow. She looked like an angel, and she took my breath away. There is nothing worse than seeing your children suffer, dark panic filling the heart with unwanted glimpses of potentially having to live without them. It is a suffocating sensation. I thought, *Dear Lord, please let her get well, let it all be good, let us go home to our family nest and tuck ourselves away into our happy place.* And God did. Eventually, she fully recovered, and now she is almost double digits, her feminine body now hinting at curves to come!

I am fully aware that children are a gift from God. Psalm 127:3–5 assures me of it: "Children are a gift from the LORD; they are a reward from him. Children born to a young man are like arrows in a warrior's hand. How joyful is the man whose quiver is full of them!" Our children came from God and we are releasing them to God little by little every day of our lives. I remember reading 1 Samuel 1:27–28 when we were first trying to start a family, and I was devastated because after two long frustrating years, I was not yet pregnant. I think I single-handedly contributed to the increased profits of companies making pregnancy tests! I was so tired of seeing a lonely red line . . . Reading about Hannah in 1 Samuel chapter one—her inability to have children, her plea to the Lord that if He would give her a son she would dedicate him to the Lord for his entire life—gave me such hope. She says, "I asked the LORD to give me this boy, and he has granted my request. Now, I'm giving him to the LORD, and he will belong to the LORD his whole life" (vv. 27–28).

I kept on reading that and praying to God for a child, boy or girl, but preferably a boy since he would be the first of his gender in my family since 1936. You may have a hard time believing this next story, but I assure you that all of it is true.

One night I had a spectacular dream . . . An angel being with human features, tall and dressed in white, woke me up and told me to trust him and to hold his hand. I did, and so together we easily emerged through my bedroom window, and soared above the quiet Californian night till we reached the ocean. I am deeply terrified of deep waters but the angel smiled, squeezed my hand, and we effortlessly glided through the ocean surrounded by a constant glow until we touched the bottom. The angel, still smiling, sifted out a luminescent oyster, opened it, and picked up a tiny white pearl and gently pushed it in my belly. He said: "God has heard your prayer." Then, I instantly woke up and knew without a shadow of a doubt that my husband and I were finally having our first baby. I have never, since then, experienced anything this divine and miraculous in nature, but my heavenly experience doesn't cease to amaze me every time I think of it!

We did have a son, full of colic, strong-willed, quick-witted, inquisitive—did I say strong-willed? He is now an almost thirteen-year-old "colicky" teenager, who is impassioned, hardworking, still strong-willed, compassionate, intelligent, and always disputative and ready to make me earn the right to parent him. I love both our kids like a mad woman, and I marvel at how fast the time goes by, as I see them roaming through the house, opening cupboards, making their own breakfast or snack, doing homework (some on the floor, some at the table), preparing their own backpacks for school . . .

A few days ago my son dressed up for a field trip to our state capital, wearing a dark suit, white shirt, and a black bow tie. Unaware that I was watching him, he was leaning against the front door, looking down reading something. He looked so big all of a sudden, and I imagined his wedding day, dressed the same, his brown hair framing his handsome face, ready to leave his home, dispatching from his childhood and launching into his manhood. Just a few years back, he was sitting against the same door crying that his socks were annoying him on the first day of kindergarten . . . All these stupid thoughts bunched together as we were ready to leave. No longer able to contain myself, tears welled up, and I had to pretend to go back to the kitchen for something I forgot. Call me irrational, neurotic—whatever you like—but I simply cannot help myself at times.

Oh, and it gets even worse, when I think of the day my baby girl will inevitably fall in love for the first time, or better yet infatuation, then into the serious kind of love—the kind she knows God has prepared for her—and then her daddy will have to give her away despite clenched fists that want to hold on . . . Just envisioning her womanly grown body wrapped in tulle and satin, as I place the veil over her beautiful face, I get instant anxiety, and my heart beats in its cage like a butterfly forcing its wings to escape from capturing fingers. Poor kid, she is innocently playing with her dolls and I'm about to pass out with grief from a vision that won't come to reality for over a decade! This is normal, right? You too must experience these kinds of crazy thoughts? I hope you said "yes."

It's not as if I don't realize that this is God's plan for most of us: ". . . A man leaves his father and mother and is joined to his wife, and the two are united as one" (Ephesians 5:31). I think of my husband's rhetorical question, "When are your parents coming to get you?" Did God really trust us to be the parents of these two marvelous creatures . . . Apparently so. These precious children are but gifts from God, and at times I fear that I love them a little too much. Jesus said for us to love Him first: 'You must love the LORD your God with all your heart, and all your soul, and all your mind.' This is the first and greatest commandment" (Matthew 22:37–38).

What if He didn't answer my prayer in healing my daughter . . . ? Would I have loved God any less, or think Him unfair and unjust . . . ? How crazy in love am I with God? Would I be as obedient as Abraham and be willing to sacrifice my own child? Do I have that kind of demented love for God? I am ashamed to admit this, but I falter in answering this question. Yes, I do love God with all my heart but I secretly hope He doesn't test me by taking my kids or my husband away from me, or me away from them. I just don't want to be separated from them too soon. Of course, this is because of my sinful nature. In the end, God comes first, and then our spouses, and then our children, and my irrational demented love should follow in that order as hard as that may be. Job's faith stood strong and he said it best:

> "The LORD gave me everything I had, and the LORD has taken it away. Praise the name of the LORD!" (Job 1:21)

Chapter 14

Me, Myselfie, and I

I think we risk becoming the best informed society that has ever died of ignorance.

—Ruben Blades

When both our children were little, they claimed some very interesting heavenly experiences. Our son was only four years old when at bed time he said to me: "Mom, today I saw a man dressed in white watching me play on the swing. He was smiling and said that I was going to have a great life."

When our daughter was three years old, she of course did not know how to read or write. I was teaching her the letters of her name just for fun, but nothing too academically involved. One day, when I was cleaning, I realized she was not with me on the bottom floor of our house. I called her a few times, when I heard tiny footsteps upstairs in her room. She eventually came running down the stairs with such excitement and showed me a piece of paper with her first name written on it.

"Wow," I said, a little confused.

"I wrote this, Mommy!"

"Honey, tell Mommy the truth. Who wrote this for you?"

"I did, but Jesus helped me."

Uhh . . . Umm . . . I gulped, and quickly ran upstairs. Of course, I saw no one there . . .

Who am I to say that both of my children did not in fact meet with Jesus? He said plain and clear: "Let the little children come to me, and do not hinder them, for the kingdom of heaven belongs to such as these" (Matthew 19:14 NIV). Jesus loves the children so much, possibly because they are the closest to heaven on earth. Even though we are all born with a sinful nature, they are still full of pure, clear, modest, unsoiled faith. It has not yet occurred to them to litter their minds and souls with pride or preoccupation of self . . . The very sad part about these stories is that I am the only one still remembering them. My kids have no clear recollection of their own encounters. They are now much older and they are tainted by discovery of self and its importance.

Last week, I saw my soon-to-be nine-year-old daughter take a "selfie" in the mirror. Double negative for me. I ran as if to save her from a fire and "rescued" her from, what I believe, harming herself: "No need for selfies, please. Go find something productive to do with your time. Go read, draw, write, play outside, jump on the trampoline, play in the mud, and go bother your brother, anything, but no selfies!"

I should not have overreacted because she is going to want to take selfies now even more since Mom forbids it!

Definition of "selfie": "A photograph that one has taken of one's self, typically one taken with a smart phone or web cam and shared via social media" (*Oxford Dictionary American English*).

Origin of the word "selfie": early twenty-first century. The first known selfie was taken by a photographer Robert Cornelius in 1839 which was "also the first photograph of a person." Interestingly enough in 1914, a thirteen-year-old Russian duchess was apparently the first teenager to send her selfie to a friend by photographing herself in the mirror.[5] (Girls!) In November 2013, the word "selfie" was announced as being the "word of the year" by *Oxford English Dictionary*. The word has an Australian origin, as in 2002 a young man in Australia fell in his drunken state, broke his lip, and then took a photo of himself, calling it the famous "selfie" and thus coining it as the word to revolutionize society's already narcissistic propensities.

It comes naturally to all of us humans to think of ourselves first, and then of others. Self-preservation is in our DNA. There are beautiful, priceless self-portraits painted by famous painters, or sculptures that reflect the likeness of someone, and I am grateful for that, for they did not have a camera at the time to capture their image. How I wish there were an actual true-to-life painting of Jesus that I could gaze upon . . .

In the book of Daniel, King Nebuchadnezzar has dreams of a golden statue as a tribute to himself. People, in general, seek pleasure and avoid pain. We bubble with urges to satisfy the self through images, food, clothing, new houses, new cars, new adventures, new stimulations that will bring us purpose, excitement, and satisfaction. So, for this reason, I think we should stay away from the selfie-driven world and teach our young children to disengage from the preoccupation with the media of selfie. I feel that if our children become inebriated by social media and selfie absorption, they will disengage entirely from hearing God's voice and being able to discern His purpose for their lives.

The app Instagram is known to have 53 million pictures tagged as #selfie. That sounds like a waste of precious time to me, for we are what we do most. Selfies have to be perfectly perfect—capturing the best version of ourselves. I don't want to look at my children's agenda, and see "one o'clock: taking selfies." Selfies promote occupation with the outward beauty, and it falsely teaches our young girls, especially, that physical appearance is the most important attribute. That will lead with dissatisfaction with themselves, harmful comparisons to others' selfies that are more attractive, sexy, desirable, thus propelling them to further fidget by their electronic device waiting to see how many "likes" they got on their skillfully prefigured version of themselves. That cannot be healthy for their volatile minds, for if their selfies were not abundantly recognized as amazing by all in cyberspace, then feelings of self-doubt set in, possibly even depression.

It may sound very extreme, but frivolous, vain, superficial, self-focused preoccupation leads our young girls and boys to feeling empty, famished for more attention, and then to more compulsive selfie-taking "proving" to the world that they are worthy of being admired and adored. Then, that will promote even more desire to impress and elicit envy on a peer "less attractive," making them jealous perhaps of not possessing the same pout, eye color, hair style, body shape, etc. Girls, already have body issue tendencies, wanting to look "perfect," so selfie-taking will only contribute to an increased obsession. I tell my kids all the time the wise words of Oscar Wilde: "Be yourself, everyone else is taken."

"The LORD does not look at the things people look at. People look at the outward appearance, but the LORD looks at the heart" (1 Samuel 16:7 NIV). I urge my son and daughter to imagine Jesus visiting our home, unexpected. If He walked into our house, what would He find us doing? Would we be proud of our actions, of our behavior, of our interests, our focus, of our invested time. . . ? God is interested very much with what we do with our precious time here on earth. He gave us gifts, skills, and talents to use to glorify Him, not to glorify ourselves.

My son has an iPhone, but I told him no selfies, unless you run into Sir Paul McCartney, and then by all means take a selfie of the two of you!

Do not misunderstand me, for I am not entirely against taking selfies within proper means. The ability to take selfies has launched a new convenience to our lives for sure. When we travel, it is much quicker to take pictures of ourselves than to ask a stranger to stop and do it. Selfies can be spontaneous and fun, capturing priceless instantaneous moments with dear friends or family members. These valuable impulsive flashes of suspended time would otherwise not be grasped and immortalized, if left at the mercy of finding our camera and searching for someone else to take the picture. Yes, selfies with others are fun, if taken for the proper reason, and not otherwise draining time away duck-facing for hours!

The self is deeply connected to our identity, our emotions, our morals, and our soul—to our essence as human beings and to our substance as individuals. When I was growing up, I obviously did not have as many photos of me as my children will have, but I had a precious commodity at my disposal: TIME. I long for my kids to realize that time is a gem designed by God to be used to advance ourselves as followers of Christ and do well around us—to be aware of others and extend a hand as much as we can. My husband tells our kids all the time a quote inspired by Warren Buffet: that in the beginning you make your habits, but in the end the habits will make you. In other words, if our children spend their time concerned with themselves, then that's where their focus will be, creating a barrier to hearing God's voice and feeling His presence.

Without guidance and limits, our children can easily become desensitized to others' needs. There is a whole world out there full of different kinds of people who rely on selfless deeds. I have to remind our two kids often to find a need and fill it—to try to take the focus off of themselves and put the importance on others. There are simple ways to make someone else's life better—I tell them, "If a friend drops a pencil, you be the one to pick it up, try to open the door for a teacher or a parent carrying goodies for a lunch meeting, help a kindergartner tie his or her shoelace, just look outside of yourselves, stay present and kind." I believe that our children should learn this way of living from a young age, so it becomes second nature to them.

Perhaps I also had innocent beautiful encounters with Jesus and angels when I was little; perhaps we all did, but we have since moved away from that tangible realm of being in God's presence. Guiding my children through the many temptations of modern media—including gratuitous selfie-taking—is a responsibility that I shoulder because I do not want further barricades that may hinder their spiritual growth or social awareness of others.

I just want Jesus to be proud of me, and my parenting choices, for I too am still a child of my Father in heaven, and so I imagine Him saying, "Good job, Roxana!"

Chapter 15

Hopscotch and Landlines

"My curfew was lightning bugs. My parents didn't call my cell, they yelled my name. I played outside, not online. If I didn't eat what my mom cooked, I didn't eat . . ."

—Fabulousquotes.com

Guess what I am tempted to reach for as soon as I wake up in the morning: my Facebook app on my smart phone. It *should* be the Word of God which I can also easily access on the same phone. "Thanks" to the same technology, now I can conveniently read both my Facebook and my Bible on the same device. So then why in the world do I think of Facebook first, and have to fight the nudge to find out how many people "liked" my post and what are my seven hundred and fifty friends are up to lately. The funny thing is that I didn't even grow up around technology, and look how easily conditioned I have become to surrender myself to my smart phone, iPad, iPod, mini iPad, Instagram, Twitter, and the list can go on.

Do you know what I long for? I long for simpler times. My generation, especially the Romanian one, didn't have any high-tech distractions. I had nothing but a small black and white television that only showed children programs on Saturdays. My apartment block had a huge playground filled with sand. After homework and chores, kids of different ages brimmed the swing sets, played on balance beams (of course as Romanians we had gymnastics beams on our playgrounds!), calloused hands hung on monkey bars, took turns on the teeter-totter, played endless tag, hide and seek, and built many sand castles out of plastic molds. On the weekends we did it all over again from morning till two o'clock in the afternoon. We all looked forward to Saturdays from two to two thirty, anticipating the most awaited episode of *Tom and Jerry*. Playgrounds quickly became deserted as we children scurried inside our apartments as if in rewind mode. I would climb two stairs at the time, running to my third-floor apartment plopping myself in front of our tiny TV, inhaling my allotted fill of childhood cartoons. For that blessed half hour, you could hear innocent laughter through the wide open windows, after which we all again poured out of our abodes on the crest of joy, innocence, and glee . . . Just reminiscing it fills my soul with happy notes. The lyrics by Keanne come to mind now: "Oh simple thing, where have you gone?"

My kids do not enjoy their childhood in the same way I did, and so in some ways I feel ill-prepared for parenting them in today's convoluted society. My mother had a much easier time, I think, keeping me entertained without the worry of electronic media lures. "Mom, I'm going out to play"—words that came out of my mouth every day, as I rushed outside to play hopscotch, at times even holding a jam and bread sandwich in my hands, hopping through the numbered squares. Game consoles, iPads, iPhones, group texting, bait my children from discovering the outdoors, from experiencing an old-fashioned childhood.

Three year ago the kids and I travelled to Romania to introduce them to their European roots. We spent most of our time in a small village away from any electronics. My mother still had our old landline telephone, and the kids were fascinated by the rotary dial, and by the very long cord that extended enough so that you could use it all over the house. I did just that, pulling the cord into my bedroom during my outspoken teen years when my girlfriends and I shared endless newfound articulated chatter. Recently, my mother retired that dinosaur and invested in a cordless phone . . . (Sigh.) But such is life it seems, out with the old and in with the new and then new*er*. The age of innocence is out and the age of constant advancement is in.

Both my kids mastered computer activities since they were little. My son moves his thumbs on the games controllers like a hummingbird flapping his wings, and he does it without looking! He also knows how to fully service our smart phones, and my daughter is savvy on downloading and managing her own games with full command of the screens and has full ability to maneuver through all the intricate games. It leaves me spellbound, actually. I literally feel dumb. Years ago when our son mentioned he was into Pokémon, I thought he meant a Reggae singer, like Poke "mon" said with a Jamaican accent! Don't judge me, for I am an immigrant, after all! It seems to me that kids mature faster, know sooner, expect more, their minds ripen quicker, and demand their independence earlier as if they are in a hurry to fast-forward their precious childhood.

So the question remains, what are we supposed to do as parents in regard to the increasingly overwhelming electronic devices, or "machines," as Bill O'Reilly calls them. Since there is no escaping them, and we are inevitably using these "machines," I thought why not look at the pros and cons to all this technology the new generation is saturated in.

Social media can become very addictive. Like I confessed earlier, I am pretty attached to my smart phone, and it tugs at my mind to check my different media outlets. You may not feel the same way, and that is good news, but I lack the self-discipline, and so although I have a free You Version Bible app—which incidentally was created by my church LifeChurch—I still have a hard time reaching for my phone to read it. I think it's because I have conditioned myself to consider my phone a source of social media, and I don't feel the same attraction toward my other devices like computer, Kindle, or iPad. Therefore, I prefer to read my actual book Bible. But it's not the same for my kids. My teenage son loves his iPhone Bible and that is just the way it is for this generation, and as long as he reads it I am ecstatic for him. However he also spends a lot of his time looking down at devices, and then engages in even more screen time playing soccer games on his computer, then ends up reading his book on Kindle. I think this new generation can easily become addicted to Facebook, Instagram, spending hours with their minds ambushed and seduced by the electronic media, further disengaging from the world around them, and from hearing God's voice. I have had to severely limit screen time and downloading of any apps for both my children. They may hate me now but will thank me later.

Being present is more difficult because of so many stimuli, and I am afraid as a parent, that our children will lack compassion and the ability to interact with others around them. God commands us in Romans 12:2 to renew our minds every single day, "Don't copy the behavior and customs of this world, but let God transform you into a new person, by changing the way you think. Then you will learn to know God's will for you, which is good and pleasing and perfect." How is it even possible for our young ones to stand still for a moment, and yield to God's voice, when there is so much static created by new and newer technology beckoning with minute-to-minute notifications? Our kids, and us, may become too worldly stimulated to make God our top priority.

And then there is texting—although it is convenient and fast, it is very addictive in nature for the young minds, and of course very dangerous when driving. In a way you could say that our teens are driving under the influence of texting, inebriated by the tempting *bing* noise that compels them to pick up their phone at any cost and look down to read a trivial message posing as some life-changing information. Seriously, I will have to be sedated when my kids start driving! I never text and drive, so as not to set a bad example for my children, even though I am tempted to reach for my phone when I hear a text come in. I honestly believe I get a chemical release, like an addict, when I hear the *bing* call out to me. My reflex is to look down, and I have to fight the "I just have to know" urge each time. Those tiny electronic words control our lives it seems. A young girl hit my car a while back because she was texting and driving! The enticement to look down at texts is enormous for most of us, but even more so for our kids whose lives are mainly discussed on social media.

This type of media immersion can make our children less focused, unable to engage in conversations, more tired, even more aggressive. There have been numerous studies that connect excessive video game playing, overuse of screen time, reading nonstop feeds on Facebook, Instagram, etc., to becoming short-tempered, irritable, ill-disposed, and bored. When both of my children are engaged in sports, piano lessons, or playing outside with friends, they are always more relaxed, pleasant, and patient. Two weeks ago schools were closed due to snow, and yes,

I let the kids watch TV more than usual, play on their devices longer than otherwise allowed, but it was too cold to go outside to play, so there you have it. I did what I preach against. As a result I got a lot of stomping up the stairs, doors shut to recoil back into their electronic world, eyes narrowing me or rolled into the ceiling, abundant arguing, and bickering. I am not saying that these things don't happen normally, but I noticed that excessive exposure to screen time propels them to increased frustration and untamed disrespectful behavior. All of their devices are turned over at the end of the day to us and returned the next day accordingly. Their rooms need to be free of any stimulation when they are going to bed. Instead of being asleep, I could see the "tell-tale" phone light betraying my son's promise of actually going to bed when he was told. Now, none of that.

In general, I notice that the new generation has an entitlement problem, feeling more emboldened and unafraid to speak back to their parents or their elders. It had never occurred to me to raise my voice to an offensive decibel when speaking to my mom. Don't you worry; I spoke my mind and said a few things to her in my room by myself, but *never to her face.* I don't know why, maybe because I knew she worked beyond hard to provide as a single parent and perhaps that awareness compelled me to restrain my anger.

I believe due to influence of peers, social media, and modern cultural messages, our children feel more audacious and then self-permit a certain eligibility to promote early independence. It is like a societal cue they get from one another. I see it when I go on school trips, during sleepovers, and even at church. At their age, I did not have the courage to speak my mind to my elders.

Okay, so one other thing. Be very mindful of the many smart phone apps, and check your child's texts and their other media accounts. There are a plethora of dangerous ones like Snapchat, a photo messaging app where instant photos, videos, or messages can be sent for a limited amount of time (5–10 seconds), and then they delete themselves. This offers a fertile platform for "sexting" since it is immediately erased and parents can't find anything out. I check my son's phone for any inappropriate behavior. He gets upset, accusing me of "invasion of privacy," but I tell him, "Sweetheart, you have no privacy at your age. You get it when you move out and provide for yourself." I assure him that I trust him, but at their volatile age I don't trust his peers and their influence on each other.

I read a very helpful article posted by *conservativetribune.com* informing parents of different sex codes and other private codes that are meant to leave parents in complete ignorance. Here are a few examples, but I will include the entire list at the end of this chapter:

PIR—parent in room
PRON—porn
8—oral sex
IPN—I'm posting naked
POS—parent over shoulder

Phew!! This is exhausting! Now, on a positive note, social media has made our lives easier in certain ways. Personally, I am thankful I have Facebook, because it enables me to keep in touch for free with my Romanian friends and family. With instant messaging we can conquer the thousands of miles of distance and reach each other in seconds. It is a miracle for me! Also Facebook is perfect for sharing our hurts and joys, and reaching out to our community of friends, obtaining encouragement and support. After my car accident, I asked for prayer and was overwhelmed by the outpouring of love and offers of emotional and physical help. People from Australia, Italy, Romania, and Canada knew about my plight and plea. It honestly helped my healing.

If your child has Facebook, you can see on a daily basis what they are up to, Also, I found, that due to maddening hormones, it is easier for my son to reach out to me in apology via texting. Of course, talking face-to-face is best, but I remember writing letters of remorse to my mom as well. On the brink of teenage-hood, it is hard to express the multitude of feelings and emotions in person, so I appreciate any conversation and interaction from my children, even if it's via text.

Road trips are definitely more manageable since various tablets offer instant viewing of movies and shows. Yes, I'd rather my kids read a book in the back seat, but hey, who am I kidding! Also cumbersome paper maps no longer cover the dash while driving. Your young but very capable back-seat copilot can read electronic maps for you. We say, "Son, find us the best way to get to Florida from Nashville." Or "Sweet girl, look up nearby restaurants for our next stop." They love it, we love it. Awesome.

I say if you can't beat them, then join them. Nowadays is way easier to keep tags on the whereabouts of your child. Like I already mentioned, it is super convenient to snoop on your child via Facebook, Instagram, etc. If the kids know you are reading their posts, they tend to "trim" their posts of any inappropriate language or not post so much stuff altogether. My son actually went off Instagram completely, knowing I have an account as well. He-he!

I also pleasantly discovered that both my kids share Bible verses through texts to encourage their friends. Same goes for our church Life group. We find it extremely effective to quickly text each other prayer requests, and offer instant support to one another.

Recently (and you will love this one), I discovered at www.parent. com an article called "10 Best Apps for Paranoid Parents." Since I wear that title proudly, my favorite app is Find My Kids—Footprints, which allows parents to know where their kids are at all time. Sorry, but peace of mind far outweighs the creepiness! Family Tracker is another great one, especially useful when visiting Disney Parks and everyone wants to do different things. If you have teens, this next one is worthwhile. It's called SecuraFore, which tells the parent how fast your child is driving and keeps tabs on all destinations. I will for sure subscribe to this one in three years and then in six years. My poor kids . . . I hope one day they will understand it was all done in the name of love!

We have no choice but to adapt to our advanced society yet not convert to it—everything should be about moderation and tight supervision. We take the good, discard the bad, and make the best of it! I know I can't shelter my children from our current cultural rhythm, but I *can* guide them through it. I am trying to stop them from looking down too much and instead to look around. There is an entire world out there waiting to be discovered, with majestic beauty created by God. There are people out there hurting and needing our help. It is harder to be perceptive of others while we are self-involved with our eyes in cyberspace. I tell my kids that it is less likely they will notice someone holding back tears of hurt if they are looking down, buried in senseless electronic feeds.

Our life-given moments are short, so go out and buy some colorful chalk and teach your kids how to hopscotch! Oh my . . . I hope they don't already have an app for that too!

FURTHER INFORMATION ON TEXTING CODES:
PIR—parent in room
CU46—see you for sex
53X—sex
9—parent watching
99—parent gone
THOT—that hoe over there
420—marijuana
SUGARPIC—suggestive or erotic photo
PRO—porn
8—oral sex
IPN—I'm posting naked
DOC—drug of choice
GNOC—get naked on camera
CID—acid
BROKEN—hung over from alcohol
KOTL—kiss on the lips
(L)MIRL—let's meet in real life
TDTM—talk dirty to me
LH6—let's have sex
WTTD—want to trade pictures
GYPO—get your pants off
KPC—keeping parents clueless

Chapter 16

Eeyore and Tigger

A wise person truly said, "It ought to be as impossible to forget that there is a Christian in a house as it is to forget there is a ten-year-old boy in it."
—Roger J. Squire

Ten years ago, when our son was three years old, I took him to his room for an afternoon nap. He resisted naps every single day holding on to the rails as I carried him up the stairs. I kissed him on his pudgy red cheeks and quickly went downstairs to call my sister-in-law from Canada. Finally I had a minute to myself and looked forward to some adult conversation. I went to my bedroom, where it was the coolest in the house to enjoy my phone call. After twenty minutes I hear repetitive running in the kitchen. It turns out, my boy refused to sleep, opened the freezer, took out an ice cream cone, and smeared it all over his body and . . . how should I put this as wholesomely as possible . . . he stuck the cone over his privacy, running in circles saying: "This feels sooo good!"

That was our vibrant son, and on a daily basis we had to brace ourselves for what was coming up next, for he was truly unpredictable, willful, complicated, clever, funny, and stubborn all in one day! Then, when he turned four we gave him a little sister. She was peaceful, quiet, relaxed, rarely cried, and was easy going. He called her his "fluffy pillow," and became her biggest fan and protector. When visitors came by to see our new baby, he sat at the door with a hand sanitizer pump making sure everyone was "fit" to touch his little sister.

Many of you have more than one or two children, and naturally you've realized how different your kids can be from one another. I am not at all trying to compare my two children to one another; I am merely trying to explain my aggravation when my parenting skills work on one child but not on the other. There are days when I feel ill-equipped to parent, am certain I am doing everything wrong, and that I am ruining my kids' chances at a normal life!

No two children are alike—each with unique tendencies, temperaments, habits, hobbies. Some are born strong-willed, and some more calm and placid. Dr. James Dobson's words give me relief: "Willfulness is built into the nature of some kids. . . . Children don't start life at the same place."[6]

In my case, I've basically had two characters from *Winnie-the-Pooh* living in our house: Eeyore and Tigger. As silly and emboldened as our son is, growing up he was a worrisome child, seeing his glass half empty most of the time. He was the kind of kid who at bedtime suffered from instant ailments: "I have a headache, my stomach hurts, my leg hurts, what are these brown spots on my arms (freckles, honey), I think I have a fever . . ." Despite my assurance that he is completely healthy, he would worry and worry. He doesn't know this even now (he-he), but I went to the vitamin store and bought homeopathic tablets, colored purple and white intended for boosting the immune system, and I would give him the purple one for headache, and white one for stomachache. I pulled the placebo effect on him, but as long as I did *something* about his "ailments," he would relax. We would pray about his agitation and anxiety, kiss him on the forehead, and I would say to him:

"Sweetheart, for now, give your worries a rest and go to sleep."

"Can I worry again tomorrow, Mommy?"

"Oh, honey . . . I'd rather you not, because God has your life under control, but if you must worry, better do it tomorrow . . ."

It is strange, but in a way the hope of worry gave him peace. He reminded me of Eeyore—the gloomy donkey from *Winnie-the-Pooh*—who was pessimistic and always expecting things to go wrong in his life: "I'll probably catch it too"—talking of someone else's cold—or "If it is a good morning, which I doubt."[7]

Later on, when his sister bloomed into her own personality, she aggravated her brother with her constant, always-in-a-cheerful-mood attitude. She was Tigger from the same book—never walked, but rather skipped places, always singing, and content in whatever situation she was in. She fit Todd Snider's lyrics to the song "Slim Chance": "I found a four-leaf clover in my yard today / It had one leaf missing off it, but that was okay." Incidentally, she would literally find four-leaf clovers all the time!

The weekends were the worst, when both kids were home all day, and their personalities collided, and fireworks sparked high. The son, by now ten years of age, would wake up on Saturday morning really sad and frustrated: "Ugh! I hate the weekends! There's nothing to do! We never do anything fun!" (Not true, and not true.) We couldn't afford sports every single season, or other extracurricular activities, so being at home felt like nothing to do to him. Poor Eeyore . . . nothing to do . . . and no hope of things getting better . . . His sister would be playing with her "dollies," singing and having elaborate conversations with her imaginary friends: Challaga, Lyofie, and Potatoe. (That very thing annoyed her brother in the first place!) My son would come down the stairs and plop himself on the couch, slouching in defeat, and sighing heavily over and over until we noticed. Oh, we noticed!

"Why don't you get dressed for the day, son, and go outside play," my husband would suggest.

"I don't want to do that."

"It's a beautiful day. Come help me clean the garage then."

"Noooo . . . I want to do something exciting."

"We will, but we have some weekend chores."

"I'll go help you clean the garage, Daddy!" the then-six-year-old offers, with a quick "I'm better than you" smirk directed at her brother.

He squints his face at her, and mocks her previous words. She gives him a pointed look, and mocks him back. Worse yet (for him), she starts to sing louder and louder, faking utter happiness.

"Mom! Tell her to stop singing! She is so annoying!"

"I can't help it if I'm happy," she responds with phony innocence and laughs at her very frustrated brother.

"Stop laughing, stop singing, and go to your room if you want to do any of these things!" he now yells at her.

"Stop yelling at me! You are so mean!" (As if she didn't contribute.)

The brother shows mock exasperation and concern, which instigates more anger in her. She lunges at him with her little fists, and now it is his turn to laugh. He got what he wanted: an activity for a boring Saturday—feeding off conflict and enjoying it!

You may ask why we didn't intervene during all this. That's because my husband was cleaning out the garage and I was getting ready to go grocery shopping, where I would have to take both of the kids along, so their father can work in peace. Now, let me just say that I would rather have a root canal without anesthesia than go to the supermarket full of people ready to judge my parenting skills or lack thereof. Trust me, I was the judger (not easy to admit), before I had kids: "That mom has no clue what she's doing. Her kids are running around and she's not doing anything about it!" I realize now, that she was probably beyond frustrated, tired of all the warnings of different threats, of physically separating the children, of being ignored, and gave up, wanting to just get her food and get out!

My own two lovelies would do the same thing. As the slick automatic glass opened wide, the fun would start:

"I call pushing the cart!" The brother claimed his triumph.

"Yes, but only for a while. Then it is your sister's turn."

Eventually (meaning not even five minutes), the girl would announce: "It's my turn to push!"

Her brother wouldn't budge out of the way, still holding on to the cart firmly:

"But I just got it! Mom, it's not fair!" (Poor Eeyore.)

"Well, honey, she's younger, so be kind and let her push for a while."

He reluctantly does, but as the six-year-old sister starts pushing, he places his hand on the side of the cart. I see a taunting smile tugging at the corner of his mouth, waiting for her explosive reaction which of course arrives very quickly:

"He's touching the cart!"

"You two, stop fighting, stop touching the cart, stop complaining, and stop looking at each other!"

No, no. It gets worse. The power struggles unleashes. She shoves him, he shoves her, the cart jerks around, and onlookers' eyes are narrowing at me in pretend understanding. *Bless her soul* . . . I grab the cart, frustrated and angry, but to no avail, as they are still bickering and elbowing each other, arguing back and forth. Heat rises to my head, and I feel like screaming. More people are looking, judging stares betraying their mock smiles. I warn my kids that they will be punished when we get home, but—who am I kidding?—by that time other misbehaviors will have taken place that will need punishing as well, so I will probably not follow through, forgetting the initial cause of their intended reprimand that started it all! As stress cripples my body, I feel overwhelmed and want to leave the store without ANY groceries! But, it turns out that I am the parent, and I have to stay strong and do something about the madness.

Kids get easily embarrassed, especially by their parents, and so my ten years of dancing lessons come into use, and that is exactly what I start doing. I move ahead of the shopping cart, and I start to dance, not gently, but eschewing all decorum I bust a move, bringing out Zumba and hip-hop moves. My kids' jaws drop to the floor and they freeze in complete shock. The people on the cereal aisle are looking again, but this time it is "this woman needs help" kind of stares. My children are mortified as they quickly follow me with the cart. (They are now both pushing.)

"Mom, what are you doing?" my son whispers.

"I'll stop dancing, if you two stop arguing and misbehaving."

"Mom, everyone is looking and smiling . . ."

"I don't care!" I say happily. I have the power now. (He-he.)

"We'll obey. Just stop dancing," they both plead.

Since that faithful day, dancing is what I do when I need them to behave in a public place. It has worked. Every. Single. Time.

Now, different dynamics have evolved, morphing into impatient teen hormones, testosterone-saturated outbursts, a lot of female tears, hyperactive emotions, and many different personalities from both children. Eeyore and Tigger have long faded into the childhood realm, only to be replaced by preadolescent Hulks. I never really know which kid I am going to tap into on a daily basis—the kind, sweet, loving ones, or the quick-tempered hostile ones. Either way, I have to be ready and fully armed with PATIENCE and wisdom to choose my battles carefully. When they were younger they sought each other's company albeit in conflict or harmony, whereas now it's more like, "Get out of my room!" "Yeah, okay, whatever," "I don't care," "Just leave me alone!"... (Sigh) ... Parenting is hard.

I turn to God *every day* and I pray for my children to be kind, compassionate, and loving. It makes me kind of sad inside when I see them so apart right now, playing with their own separate group of friends, having sleepovers, living parallel to each other, and not interacting as much as they used to. I cannot believe I am saying this, but I kind of miss their bickering and provoking. At least they interacted on a daily basis! I am sure this is a normal stage (other parents tell me it is), and that soon they will be close friends. I am the only child, so sibling intimacy is important to me.

It never ceases to amaze me how well God knows His people, and how He filled the Bible with such incredible advice, foreseeing our need to know and understand how to parent and raise godly children. I love it how aware and intentional He is about explaining to us that each child He makes comes to us with their unique personalities, and He intends to use that for His glory. Then, God counts on us, the parents, to nourish and channel their individuality (no matter how frustrating it is), and to shepherd them through His precious guidance. The Amplified Bible explains it well in Proverbs 22:6, "Train up a child in the way he should go [and in keeping with his individual gift or bent], and when he is old he will not depart from it."

God knew my two children before I knew them. He was fully aware of my son's "Eeyore" tendencies, his impassioned strong will, but also of his compassion, intelligence, and philosophical depth. God took delight in creating my daughter, with her skipping gait, cheerfulness, wisdom, but also her fretfulness.

God also knew *your* children before you met them. Ephesians 2:10 reassures us that "we are God's masterpiece. He has created us anew in Christ Jesus, so we can do the good things he planned for us long ago." I literally get goose bumps when I read the word "masterpiece." It moves me to realize that we are all God's supreme piece of work, His opus,

His outstanding best creation. Each one of us was a child at one point, and each generation is accountable for the next. It freaks me out a little thinking of the responsibility we have with these two marvelous gifts God entrusted us with, and that is why I ask myself often, "When are their parents coming to get them?" Then I realize with ecstatic joy and humble relief the most cherished answer: never.

Chapter 17

"What Now?!"

A child needs to be hugged and unhugged. The hug lets her know she is valuable. The unhug lets her know she is viable. If you are always shoving your child away, they will cling to you for love. If you are always holding them closer, they will cling to you for fear.

—Billy Graham

"Mom! Mom! Mom!" I couldn't wait for my little darlings to start calling me "Mom," and now I hear it in exceeding abundance.

"Mom, where are my hair clips? I need my hair to be perfect like Jen's. She said her mom does it." *Well, her mom probably wakes up an hour before her kids do, makes perfect breakfast, and perfect hair. I sleep in as much as I can. I hope you don't become best friends with Jen, cause then I'll have to meet her mom and feel bad about myself!*

"Where is my phone!? I left it right here. Did you move it when you cleaned?" *Yeah, I cleaned. What a foreign concept!* "Mom, you need to sign my school papers." "Mom, I need more money for the cafeteria." They even call me when I go to the bathroom, as if until then there was no "pressing" emergency (no pun intended. Ha-ha!). I cannot even pee in peace; little notes are being pushed under the door (mainly by my daughter), with questions or messages. Ugh!!!

"Mom, there are no more waffles." "Mom, you know I don't like the gluten-free ones with blueberries. . ." *There are starving children around the world who would love gluten-free anything.* "Mom, I can't find my shoes." "Mom, don't forget today is tryouts for soccer." *Oh, yes, the new sport we are trying out!* "Mom, you are coming to the middle school concert right?" *Ugh! I forgot about that!* "I need dress shoes for it by the way." (He tells me this the morning of the concert. Sigh.) "Mom, my gymnastics leotard is too small for me. I need a new one." *Of course you do. Why don't I just staple my credit card to my forehead?* "Mom, can I have a sleepover at Drake's house this weekend?" *Well, I don't know, it's just Monday, only the first day after the last weekend.* "Mom, my bike helmet is too small." "No-no, I bought you a new one," I remind him. "That one, Mom . . . Really? I'm thirteen; I need something cooler, and I don't wear camouflage anymore." Of course he's thirteen now (at the time I was writing this chapter he turned a teen) . . . (Sigh again.) "No fair, Mom. If he's going to a sleepover, can I have a sleepover with Bella then?" *Has anybody heard me say "yes" to either of them? Didn't think so.* "Mom, can I not do all my chores now. There are too many . . ." *Well, can I not feed you every single day?*

The matriarch title is an important one—evoking the mother being the ruler of a home, or a dignified woman, or my favorite: a dowager. Yes, indeed, ranking me with the likes of Downton Abbey aristocracy! However, I must humbly admit that I feel fatigued at times by the many responsibilities that go along with the title. I lay my head on the kitchen counter when my kids call "mom" one more time. "What now?!" I ask, overwhelmed as I brace myself. Then my daughter simply says, "Nothing. I just wanted to say I love you so much. You are the best mommy ever!" Waves of guilt wash over me, my emotions awakened to the privilege and preciousness of being called "Mom."

A teacher of mine, Dr. David Walley, once said, "Never let parenting become an inconvenience." Isn't *that* the truth, at least for me. My husband sometimes jokes by saying that we didn't know what happiness was until we had kids, and then it was too late! Of course entirely not true, but parenting is extremely challenging on so many levels, especially if you are rearing your children in a Christ-centered home. My pastor says that our purpose is to raise fully devoted followers of Christ. Well, that's easier said than done in our emancipated society, filled with non-traditional, unconstrained values and morals. Throw in the many electronic distractions and a moody non-deciphering teenager and the frustration begins.

My now nine-year-old girl still wants us to hug her, carry her to bed, loves piggyback rides, cuddles forever, and absorbs our affection like a sponge. I am not sure how long it will last but I'll take it as long as she gives it. On the other hand, the brooding youngster with a constant disputative expression etched on his face, acts like WE are the inconvenience to his life. I find it difficult to read his feelings, as he is very selective with how much he shares with us. (I hear that's normal.) For instance, the other evening he and I watched a great movie together called *The Greatest Game Ever Played*. It was rated G which invoked frowns, "ugh" noises, and frustrated rolling of his eyes. He thinks because he is "older" now it is somehow "beneath" his maturity to succumb to the G rating which, in my opinion, sometimes can stand for "godly." I told the anxious teen that if he doesn't like the movie after twenty minutes we'll stop it. An hour went by and not only did he not want to turn it off, but he indulged me with the "highly endangered due to extinction" head on my lap. My back was killing me from sitting in the same position for too long, but there was NO WAY I was going to shift and take the risk of him moving off of me . . . So, I barely watched any of the movie, basking in the disbelief of my teenage son letting me hold him. It may sound silly, but for any adoring, affection-starved mother this was a HUGE deal.

After the movie was over, I said a quick "Good night"—as too much lingering would pop the affection bubble—but then he motioned me with his head toward his room. After he hugged his dad, he whispered to me, "Come to my room for a second." I followed him. With his back to me he gets in bed as I emotionally rub my palms together in anticipation of having a possible intimate conversation with my son. Why else would he motion me so discreetly to his room? I sit gently on the side of his mattress when he says,

"Mom, what are you doing?"

"You told me to come to your room."

"No, I didn't."

"Uhh . . . yes, sweetie, you did."

"No, I didn't. Why did you follow me into my room?"

Oh my goodness! I feel like Marlin from the *Finding Nemo* movie, following after the short-term-memory Dory . . .

"Okay, son. My bad. Good night. I love you." I leaned to give him a hug and a head kiss.

"Mom! Don't hug me . . . Just . . . I don't know . . . Good night."

"Okay." I blew him a kiss and walked away.

"Mom! So you're not gonna hug me at all?"

Oh my!! "You just told me not to hug you, honey."

"Yes, hug. No kiss."

I hugged the conflicted teenager, who is growing up so fast and trying to detach himself from his mother, but he is not quite fully ready . . . Seriously, this child needs to discover a cure for a disease or something else amazing like that, for all the aggravation he's putting me through. And then he has to thank me in front of a lot of people from a podium as he receives his award. Chocked up with unbearable gratitude, he singles me out in the audience and he says, "My mother . . . She's the reason I am here today." Of course I look fabulous at fifty as people applaud and I soak in the adoration. Strictly fantasy, of course, as my husband is an awesome influence in his life as well, but this book is not about him. It's about me.

In reality, I have no true grasp on what went on that night, but my guess is that he really did have something to tell me, but he changed his mind. He probably felt uncomfortable of the sudden intimacy required to share his thoughts and emotions. At this pubescent age, he is ambushed by irritated, charged hormones eating away at his sense of logic like Pac-Man. The mere fact that I gave birth to him probably mortifies him right now!

Poor kid, it doesn't help that he has a European mother who loves to laugh out loud, makes soulmates with strangers at the store, uses her hands to punctuate her many sentences, and hugs mostly everyone she meets. Lately he actually sat me down and talked to me in bullet points:

Mom,

- Don't run across the soccer field to give me water.
- Don't say "Hi" to my friends.
- Drop me off at the corner for Wednesday night church.
- Don't ask me too many questions right after school. I'm tired and I've had a long day.

- At night before bed, I can cuddle with you on the couch during the *O'Reilly Factor*. You can hug me, pinch my cheeks, but not before that time.
- I know you love me, and I love you too, but I need some space now. I have too many hormones to deal with.
- Don't hug me in public, unless I hug you first.

I must say, over all, a very poised articulation of his requests, and I have to admit not too unreasonable for a teenager. He spoke. I listened. We agreed. (Although his friends think I am a cool mom!)

At least my son prepares me for dealing with his sister when she becomes a teen. For now the only things she is stressed about is going to school. She frets like a frightened Chihuahua: "I'm scared I didn't do my homework right." "I think I forgot something at home." "What if I don't remember anything I studied?" "What if I 'clip down' on the behavior chart?" She is hyper-conscious and worries about doing the right thing, and being the best at what is expected of her. I wish I could make her understand that this is just a season in her life and it will all pass and that she has a beautiful long life ahead of her. I ask her something I read in a book once, "Have you ever seen a stressed-out flower?" I explain to her that God is with her—with all of us—all of the time. He cares about what happens to her and what she worries about, and He wants her to have peace and trust Him in all situations. I read to her Luke 12:27, "Consider how the wild flowers grow. They do not labor or spin" (NIV). Only *we* toil and spin over the details of our lives. I cannot blame my girl too much, for apparently this is genetic . . . Yes, I was (and still am at times) the same way. We pray every morning on our way to school for God to give her peace, to calm her anxious heart, and to reassure her of His loving presence.

I teach both the children the same positive statements I tell myself, "God is good all the time." "Today will be a great day." "God has a great plan for my life." "Every day is a gift." "Be kind, make a difference." Growing up is hard, parenting is challenging, but life is a gift from God and is filled with hardships but also wonder and beauty. Honestly, I don't how people raise their children without God and the church. I depend on God every minute, and my church has been instrumental in helping with both the kids. When our son seems aloof with issues, and won't talk to us, he reaches out to his pastor, who always makes time to listen to him, gives him precious advice, and prays with him. Our daughter's Wednesday night teacher encourages her weekly, filling her soul with encouragement, and nurtures her talents at all times. Both children receive special cards in the mail, sent by youth pastors, expressing their love for them, and how impressed they are with their godly character.

The girl cherishes those cards, and the boy does mutter under his breath, "Yeah, that's really cool." I, too, look forward to reading those supportive words, for it gives me relief that we are not alone in this parenting thing. It relaxes me to know that I have people out there loving on my kids.

As I said earlier, I do get frustrated, overwhelmed, and question my fitness as a mother, thinking I have not been my very best at my mothering skills, but I try to lean on God to help me bring up Christ-centered children, and then I thank Him for the high honor of being a mother.

Wendy's words in the movie *Peter Pan* move me to tears when I think of them. She describes a mother as ". . . the most wonderful person in the world, she's the angel voice . . . that bids you good night . . . ask your heart to tell you her worth, your heart will say heaven on earth, another word for divine, your mother and mine."

Chapter 18

If You Don't Stand for Something, You'll Fall for Anything

Teach your children to choose the right path, and when they are older, they will remain upon it. (Proverbs 22:6 TLB)

When I was fourteen years old I knew *way* more than my mother. I was exponentially smarter than she was, I had a keen awareness of what was best for my life, ignored all her nagging advice, thought she was old-fashioned, frustrating to be around, and she asked too many questions I already had answers for—not to mention she was often an inconvenience to my hard-earned independence. I do hope this sounds familiar, or I was a very bad daughter! It was just the age when I drifted apart most from my only parent, and it ended up hurting me in so many ways . . .

I remember I lied to her about going to a two-hour math tutorial (never my best subject), for which my mom payed money we didn't have. Instead I chose to hang out with the wrong crowd for those two hours. I was so stupid to think that my tutor wouldn't call my mom to inform her of my absence! When I came home, my mother was sitting alone at the dining room table in complete silence, with her head buried in her palms. She didn't say anything, she just looked up at me with such hurt and pain in her eyes that it somehow helped me to fully realize that I was actually doing the wrong thing with my life.

American politician Alexander Hamilton is known for saying, "Those who stand for nothing will fall for anything." Yep, indeed. But that is insanely hard to teach to our children right now because as Sheryl Crow sings, "These are the days when everything goes." Our current culture is laced with the posture of, "Well, if it feels good then do it." My kids would sure love to live by this motto right now, but their dad and I are in the way.

Then what should we want our children to stand for? Personally, I want my kids to stand for honesty, kindness, compassion, integrity, godliness—all the values that we should all possess. But there are three things that I would despise for my son and daughter to represent: entitlement, laziness, and sexual impurity.

These are prime times for our children to easily become entitled. There is so much stuff to want left and right with the temptation of accumulation everywhere,

"Mom, Scott has an iPod 5 and he just got the new iPhone 6."

"Well, that's great for him, but your old iPod is perfectly fine, and there is no need to obsess with newer things which soon will become old things."

"Mom, you're making no sense."

"I know, but trust me; I know what's best for you."

"Ugh! It's not fair!"

Well, life is not fair, and having more stuff doesn't *make* it fair. (Sigh . . .) I am trying to teach both our children to work for what they want, and to learn the precious value of earning it themselves. In fifth grade our son wanted to go on a school trip to Memphis, and so we decided as a family that he could help pay for it. He started mowing one neighbor's yard, raked leaves for another, and little by little he earned half the needed cost. He felt pretty proud of himself and enjoyed his trip even more! I tell both the kids that there is no substitute for hard work. You either do it or you don't.

Believe it or not, we are all born determined. It is not in our nature to start life by giving up. Babies are very tenacious and diligent at screaming and crying as long as it takes until they are fed and changed, or later when they start crawling they are determined to reach the toy they want. They will stand strong until their needs are met.

The same determination should be applied when they are older toward self-discipline, and as parents we must encourage our children at all times, to stand for the right things in life yielding to God' Word and guidance. Bill O'Reilly said this once as the tip of the day during his program: "Self-discipline is formed by not giving into adversity. If you can do it, do it."

There are plenty of opportunities for our teenage son to combat adversity of idle hands. He can mow the grass, help fix the fence, help Dad build the deck, teach piano to his sister, wash the car, referee for soccer games, and the list can go on. We are paying him for his hard work so he can learn the connection between dedication and reward. Then comes the lesson on tithing, which is hard to apply after just making a bit of money, but he quickly learned that God blesses him with more opportunities for work, good health, and great friends. Actually he told us he really feels God's blessing on his life when he is generous with his earnings. Yep. God is good like that.

The same goes for his sister. Right now she has a list of chores printed on the fridge to which she abides for free. I grew up in a country where kids did not have the opportunities to earn money. There was no freedom of entrepreneurship, no matter how old you were. You worked because you earned a degree. I thank God for all the advantages my children have at their disposition. The Bible is filled with verses on hard work, dedication, perseverance, and self-discipline. I love the frankness of Proverbs 10:4, "Lazy people are soon poor, hard workers get rich."

As I mentioned already, while writing this book, our son turned thirteen, and just like that he changed into a quiet, morose, hard-to-understand human being. It feels as though he kept careful sentinel to the clock in his room and when the last minute of his twelfth year stitched into the new minute of his thirteenth year, he thought, *Yay, I'm thirteen now! I can ignore my parents, furrow my brows at everything they say, answer their questions with grunts and shrugs, forever plug my ears with headphones, keep my room door closed at all times because I'm a teen and I know everything!*

I understand that teenagers are full of hormones, trying to figure themselves out, that friends' opinions matter more that the parents'. I get that they seek acceptance and validation outside their home, and I realize that I have to give my son physical and mental space by not annoying him to death with all my questions. I know that I cannot reach and hug him like I used to, thus humiliating him, that I have to have infinite patience, and that I have to trust and pray that he'll be able to fight the temptation of pornography and other sexual impurities. Easier said than done. Our children have access to the internet on basically every device and a myriad of phone apps that provide ideal platforms to engage in highly inappropriate behaviors. Apps like Whisper, Yik Yak, just to name a few, enable our youth to take instant picture of their exposed selves and share it in cyberspace in seconds. Yes, when maturing kids are densely packed with erratic hormones, insecurities, lust, desire to be accepted, the antidote to all this incitement is daily Bible reading, spending time with God, and constant involvement of the parents. I tell my son that God is so cool and awesome in leaving us with ammunition to fight our sinful ways. He very specifically addresses the youth, "How can a young person stay on the path of purity? By living according to your word. I seek you with all my heart; do not let me stray from your commands. I have hidden your word in my heart that I might not sin against you" (Psalm 119:9–11 NIV).

I don't care how appalled my children may be when I check their texts, or their phone apps. Both, their father and I want to give them a perceived sense of independence, but keep a tight rein as well.

James 1:14–15 is very clear that "Temptation comes from our own desires, which entice us and drag us away. These desires give birth to sinful actions . . ." Personally, I wish for my two kids to stand for purity and abstinence. When I was a teen, and went out with my friends, my mother would bluntly say to me as I was going out the door: "Roxana, always protect your vagina!" *Really?* Yes. Really. I wanted to die and cringed every time she shamelessly articulated such abominable advice to me. It was such buzzkill when I was about to go on a date with a stomach full of rousing butterflies. I guess that was exactly her intention, for her embarrassing words to hover and dilute any hormonal temptations we may have had. She insisted on God's Word on abstinence until marriage and we talked many times about it. Anyway, her incessant cautioning worked, but I am not sure I will use those exact words on my daughter. Maybe I'll yell at her as she leaves the house to protect her *heart* instead of her vagina, "Above all else guard your heart, for everything you do flows from it" (Proverbs 4:23 NIV).

In the end I think it all comes down to teaching our children to have an intimate relationship with Christ, and as a result the desire to please Him will be higher than that of pleasing themselves. That way they won't fall for just anything that will inevitably come their way, for there will be many temptations for the rest of their lives, even as adults.

I remember when the book *Fifty Shades of Grey* came out I was tempted to read it. I indulged in a few sample chapters on my Kindle, and I have to admit that it was tantalizing nonetheless. At the end of the samples, the yellow button asked me seductively if I "want to purchase" and I paused, thought about it for a moment as my heart *was* longing for more, but I clenched my teeth and pressed "No." Relief swept over my warm body, releasing my smothered temptation. In order to deal with my frustration and inner conflict, I wrote a blog called *Fifty Shades of Grey—A Christian Woman's Perspective*, which I will include at the end of this chapter.

Our current culture with the steadfast growth in modern technology beckons our young children, luring them into many impure media forums exposing them to ungodly temptations. The way they understand the path to righteousness will affect their future married lives. Every day at bedtime we pray for God to guide our thoughts, our words, our deeds, and we also pray for their future spouses. We ask God to guide our daughter and our son to the husband and wife He has prepared for them, for their marriages to be blessed with love, respect, honor, and devotion. I feel it is never too early to pray for the future persons my kids will spend the rest of their lives with. Soon my son will start dating girls, and eventually my daughter will have her first crush on a handsome boy, and they will come home infatuated, broken hearted, then infatuated again, and I pray they will know how to discern and choose good people to be with. I read an article by Diane Stark called "Tween Crushes" in which she says this,

When my daughter had a crush on a boy, I asked her to place his name in 1 Corinthians 13:4–6. She did. "Sean is patient and kind; Sean does not envy or boast; Sean is not arrogant or rude. Sean does not insist on his own way; Sean is not irritable or resentful; Sean does not rejoice at wrongdoing, but rejoices with the truth." She frowned. "I saw him pick on another boy in the hallway. I guess he wasn't very kind."[8]

I am definitely using this with both my kids. It is a perfect way to glean some truth on someone.

Stand for honesty, my dear children, for hard work, for purity of mind and heart, for that is the will of our Lord Jesus Christ who loves you very much.

Create in me a clean heart, O God. Renew a loyal spirit within me. . . . Restore to me the joy of your salvation, and make me willing to obey you. (Psalm 51:10–12)

Fifty Shades of Grey—A Christian Woman's Perspective[9]

Wow! What can I say . . . The reviews for *Fifty Shades of Grey*, the erotica, mature book by E. L. James, are highly controversial, as it becomes a best seller in Britain and the United States. There is a lot of increasing buzz concerning the explicit sexual content of this book, as many women around me are avidly reading it. I heard it being referred to as "mommy porn."

Friends consistently ask me if I have read it, so I went to the bookstore and looked through it. Also, after reading the sample trial on my Kindle, I have decided that *Fifty Shades of Grey* is definitely not for me as a Christian woman, wife, and mother. The male character is sadomasochistic, has a penchant for sexual violence, bondage, and hitting for erotic pleasure. Debaucheries take place in hidden dungeons, as they both subjugate each other to sexual lechery. Aside from being a love story, this book is infectious in nature for my mind and soul.

The beginning of the first book starts off captivating, even inspiring further interest in the plot. Personally, I have an impressionable mind, and passion of any kind easily takes root, but as my trial sample ended on my Kindle, I felt unsettled in spirit and polluted in emotion. It reminded me of when I read the other famous book *Twilight*, which left me depressed, discontent with my reality, and longing for young love . . . I realized that the realm of fantasy can be dangerous for me, and I have to be careful what I fill my mind with.

This is what MY OWN Christian opinion is on the following issues and presupposed questions regarding the book *Fifty Shades of Grey*:

"This book is just fiction, and it spiced up our marriage and our sex life."

Yes it is fiction, but the content is pornographic in nature and depicts explicit, excessive, twisted, graphic sexual material. It incites the temptation to fantasize about a different man other than your husband, or for another woman other than your wife. I realize this book is predominantly read by women, and from my perspective, sexual mental images about someone else are impure, illicit, and considered unfaithful. Ephesians 5:3 ordains us to "Let there be no sexual immorality, impurity among you," and verse 4 says "Obscene stories . . . these are not for you."

God wants us to stay pure and fix our thoughts on what is "true, honorable, and right" (Philippians 4:8). Reading crude, lascivious books is not pure for our hearts and minds. If you have marital problems and the contents of this book have brought you closer, what I think is that extracting your intimacy from sexual vulgarity is never healing in a marriage, nor does it offer a true solution from ongoing conflict.

As married couples, we can stem that intimacy from Song of Songs, a lyric poem inspired by God. This book in the Bible is filled with sensuous, amorous, exciting, exotic, enticing beautiful details. Chapter 4 for instance goes into great details, exploring the attraction and longing between a man and a woman. Here a few excerpts from Song of Songs: "You have ravished my heart, my lovely one, my bride; I am overcome by one glance of your eyes, by a single bead of your necklace. . . . Your lips, my dear, are made of honey. Yes, honey and cream are under your tongue" (4:9, 11 TLB). The woman is described as having lips like ribbons of scarlet, and a delicious navel. She dreams in chapter five about her lover, husband-to-be, knocking on her bedroom door saying, "Open to me my darling, my lovely doe, for I have been out in the night. My head is soaked with dew and my hair with wetness of the night." He further thinks of her rounded thighs, and she of his muscular arms and strong manly legs. Let these verses arouse a crimson color in you and spouse's cheeks . . .

God's source is a much better place for what should be beautiful intimacy. Proverbs 5:19 commands us to be "intoxicated," or "captivated" in our love for each other, and 1 Corinthians 7:3–5 says to let our bodies fill us with delight, and to satisfy one another: "So do not deprive each other of sexual relations," and "The wife gives authority over her body to her husband and the husband gives authority over his body to his wife." Sex is a blessing to a married couple, but can be detrimental if indulged in abusive ways, as described in *Fifty Shades of Grey*.

"I am a young unmarried woman, so I don't see the harm in reading Fifty Shades of Grey."

Personally, I would not let my own daughter, or son, read any kind of erotica novels, especially this one. Second Timothy 2:22 says "Run from anything that stimulates youthful lust. Follow anything that makes you want to do right." This book depicts a young, single, and graduating-from-university girl, who is seduced by a rich, attractive, well-spoken, powerful man. That is prime soil for a young heart looking to fall in love... However, he is a troubled man, with dark, impure desires, trapping her in obsessive lust, exploiting her physically and emotionally. A young woman indulging in such a novel will only become seduced by unchaste activities, by a distorted view on how love is supposed to look like, and further be allured by debaucherous narrative, imagining herself part of a realm filled with vulgar, crude sexual escapades. I am aware that there is supposed to be a "deeper" love story woven through this book and the next two sequels, but no woman should find herself attracted to a man who is sadistic, controlling, and domineering. First Corinthians 6:12 warns us: "You say, 'I am allowed to do anything'—but not everything is good for you. . . . [You] must not become a slave to anything." My advice is to go read Jane Austen books like *Pride and Prejudice*.

In the end, this is just a book written by a writer fueled by her own imagination and fantasies. Anyone can write any book they want, but we, as Christians, I believe, must be selective in what would be honoring and pleasing to God. Ask yourself if this book is bringing you closer to God, and how would you feel if Jesus showed up at your house wanting to look at your bedside book selection. I find that whatever I read ends up preoccupying my thoughts and feelings, so reading *Fifty Shades of Grey* would become addictive and lead to seeking similar books, videos, etc. Immorality originates in the mind, and Galatians 5:17 acknowledges our temptations: "The Spirit gives us desires that are the opposite of what the sinful nature desires. These two forces are constantly fighting each other, so you are not free to carry out your intentions." As Christians, it is hard to navigate through the tempting lures of this world, but we must arm ourselves with God's holy words: "Carefully determine what pleases the Lord. Take no part in the worthless deeds of evil and darkness; instead expose them" (Ephesians 5:10–11).

Chapter 19

Oh, So Many Lessons!

Making the decision to have a child is momentous—it is to decide forever to have your heart go walking around outside your body.
—Elizabeth Stone

Two years ago the kids and I got rear-ended with a strong *thud* by another car. They were shaken, of course, but physically okay. I too seemed fine but overwhelmed by the flurry of policemen, firemen, paramedics . . . It was my first accident, so I felt quite panicked inside, but tried to stay strong for the children. I thought they would be crying in shock, but they were dutifully watching from inside the car, peeking through the back window and munching on raisins. I started to smile when I saw their stuffed cheeks and curious eyes. Later, I thanked them for being so calm and obedient. They each said that God is always watching over us and that there is nothing to worry about. Ah, the faith of a child! I wish I could purchase it and enclose in pretty little bottles that say: *Pure Child Faith.* "Yes, please. I'll buy one hundred!" For them it is that easy: God is good. Done. My kids have taught me, and still are teaching me many lessons. As a parent, I'm usually the one doing the teaching, but that day I learned to trust God in a deeper way no matter how tough a situation is.

A couple of months passed, and my son modeled unwavering devotion to our Lord and Savior. As a result of the accident, I developed severe back pain, which was constant, annoying and also gnawing at my soul. I felt depressed, and I simply did not feel like going to church, and seeing happy faces full of joy, and healthy people embracing each other. I felt resentful in my agony, and unwilling to be around my fellow church members. I announced my decision to the family, but our son, then eleven years old, asserted, "Mom, you can stay home, but I'm going to church even if I have to walk or if someone else comes to pick me up. God doesn't like it when we skip church!"

Uh . . . well . . . Matthew 21:16 *does* say, "Haven't you ever read the Scriptures? For they say, 'You have taught children and infants to give you praise.'" So, with nothing left to say, and breakfast half finished, my husband rushed our kids to the car and made it to church on time. Not me. Learning nothing from my son's precious devotion, I stayed home, pulled the bed covers over my head, and wallowed in my pain. When they returned from church, my husband had a look of shock on his face, "Honey, guess what the service was about . . . It was about living with PAIN!!"

Whatever. That's not true. With an ironic smile tugging at his lips, my son quirked his eyebrows up and down and added, "I told you, Mom, you should have come to church!" Well served, son. Well served.

I do have to admit in gratitude, that both my children were extremely encouraging and prayed over my aching body for months. They never became discouraged over my condition. They taught me dedication to God's loyal character. It still moves me to tears to think back on my daughter's little hands pressed together telling God, "I know You are healing my mom, because You love her." And He did.

One year ago my husband took us zip lining, despite my lobbying against it—I am extremely afraid of heights and not an adrenaline junkie. Let's just say that while my family seeks the rollercoasters, I prefer the merry-go-round. (Don't judge.) Nevertheless, on that particular day I stood ninety feet above the ground looking down at tree tops. Apparently I was supposed to simply step off the platform into an exhilarating ride . . . I just could not do it. Fear gripped my whole being as panicked tears welled up, "Can't do it. I'm getting down." Both my children would not have it, "Mom, you can. Face your fears!" Also my son snuck in a different angle, "You are the mom, and you want to teach your children to give up?" Agh . . . this child of mine . . . So prompted by guilt and artificial courage, I let go, screamed all the way across, but I did it! That day, my kids taught me to not let fear win over me.

I praise God that my children do not struggle with the same things I have to conquer, such as fear, self-doubt, and many other "agreements," like John Eldredge calls them. Eldredge believes that we all make certain agreements with ourselves, usually about ourselves, and these will end up determining how we process the way we live and function every day. For instance, I also struggle with fear of abandonment, and that I am not very capable or have any worthwhile abilities. Growing up I didn't get the best grades in school like some of my "able," smarter friends; therefore, false belief sprouted in my heart and self-doubt became a constant parasite. My father left us when I was born, and so I felt abandoned my whole life—false agreement stamped on my heart that if my earthly father doesn't love me, how can a heavenly father, whom I don't see, care about me . . . Because of this fear I struggle with the anxiety of losing my loved ones . . .

I realize that the enemy likes me swimming in these destructive agreements until my fingers get "pruney," so to speak. I don't want my children to experience these types of lies.

I know I have lamented in other chapters about the kids constantly needing me, calling me every five minutes, but that's what kids want most from their parents: TIME. That is hard to produce in abundance, due to the hustle and bustle of our today's society—busy working schedules and packed after-school activities. When our son was little he used to say that Mommy lives at home and Daddy lives at work, and when my husband walked through the front door, he was always swept by our two kids in a flurry of hugs and kisses. Before he could even put his briefcase down he was fully engaged in giving the kids attention. Forget about washing hands or even going to the bathroom! A Citibank card commercial had this advertising message a while back: "Make some time that you can lose track of." Yes! And I learned that from our kids. They want our time, not our money (although my now-thirteen-year-old will debate that), and not more stuff to make up for us missing their piano recital or soccer championship.

I have realized that they are the most happy and at peace when we spend time together as a family. I am hoping that if we give them our time when they are young, they will give us their time later on in life. At times, my son and I make dinner together, and I even let him prepare the entire meal. He is always surprised by that as if he won a brand new PS4, "Really, Mom?!" Yes. Really. As we get comfortable in the kitchen, he opens up to me (which is usually rare at his age), and I get to teach him about spices, flours, sauces, and that when he goes over to his friends' houses, the most important person at the table is the mother: "Son, you can't eat until the mother sits as well, and you have to make sure to fetch her a drink. Also, help with dishes; clean up around you, especially if you sleep over there." I am hoping he will win "brownie points" with his future in-laws on the first time he goes home to meet *her* parents. (Sigh . . . That time will come . . .)

I do believe that deep inside, our children are our biggest fans, just as we rally for them on a daily basis. Our son jumps at the opportunity to go to work with his dad and watch him create all his inventions. My mother worked in a chemical lab, and all the mixing bottles and different colors fascinated me. To this day, the smell of ammonia is reminiscent of spending time with my mother at her work. My girl loves to emulate me and writes stories and books almost every day.

For a while, we the parents are their whole world, and I want them to remember us fondly. Proverbs 17:6 says, "Parents are the pride of their children." It's a generational thing, and I hope that our kids too will endeavor to be the best parents to their own children.

The hardest thing I've had to learn is to have unlimited patience with both the kids. There are times when I am in a hurry, and unfairly rush them to get in the car and to stop talking so much. I lose my temper unnecessarily and then I see their innocent faces well up with tears, so I feel like a big jerk. But there you have it. Life can be stressful, with financial responsibilities, sickness, demanding schedules, and sometimes both kids talk incessantly and my brain expands like a balloon about to pop, and all I can think about is my cold bed sheets. I literally lock myself in my room, tell the kids I need a break, and lay in the lap of cold mattress luxury, where my thoughts get cleared. Weird? Maybe, but it's the bare truth.

Our children can teach us a lot—even when it's uncomfortable for us to hear. Whenever my son would put my nerves through the grinder, I would explode and say, "What's wrong with you?!" until one time he responded, "There is nothing wrong with me, Mom." Double gulp on my side, the bricks of guilt lying heavy on my heart . . . I was the one labeling "him" as problematic rather than his behavior. God thought of this as well, "Fathers, do not provoke your children to anger by the way you treat them. Rather, bring them up with the discipline and instruction that comes from the Lord" (Ephesians 6:4). Yeah, the last thing I want is to damage my children through my lack of patience and hurtful words. I have learned to swallow my sinful pride and apologize to my children whenever I am in the wrong.

You know, I have never seen my parents in the same room. Never. I have to take their word for it that I am theirs. I don't even have a picture of the three of us together. Kind of sad for me, but God is good and He gave me a spectacular husband and father, and our two kids see us (more than they want to) kiss and silly dance around the room. Each time they catch us smooching in the kitchen, they exclaim, "Eew, gross!" but they secretly love it on the inside. It's good for them to see their parents happy and in love. Behind their mock disgust, I always see beaming faces filled with secured love.

In the past thirteen years since I have become a parent, I have learned a lot about my children and myself *from* my children. If someone were to ask me what makes a great parent, I would say: LOVE. Lots and lots of love: the tough kind, the affectionate kind, the forgiving kind, the patient kind, the unconditional kind but most of all the humble kind—the kind that can teach God's truth through a child.

Parenting never ends, not even when my kids will be fifty and I will hopefully make it to eighty. It is full-time and it's for life, and I feel ecstatic knowing that I am spending my life molding another.

Chapter 20

The Memory Room

Children are not a distraction from more important work.
They are THE most important work.

—C. S. Lewis

Despite having a very comfortable family room, we all end up huddling in the kitchen around a small wooden island. This reminds me of my own childhood and of our vast family get-togethers, everyone congregating in the "kitchen house," which my grandparents built as a separate building but connected to their main house. Again, regardless of many other spacious rooms, we all preferred that kitchen, which I fondly refer to as the "memory room."

My grandparents' house tucked away in a small, bucolic Romanian village was most definitely the place where everyone ran for comfort, food, emotional refuge, wisdom, acceptance, love, basically everything. It defined us as a family, and the kitchen is where it all took place.

Christmas was exceptionally memorable. I remember anxiously awaiting the arrival of my uncles, boisterously walking through the kitchen door, brushing snow off their clothes, and instantly filling up the space with volume and laughter. My mom and aunts were busily sharing news as they wrapped aprons around their hips ready to help my grandmother with holiday cooking. We cousins climbed hills full of snow, came down on sled rides, and bounced through the front door red-cheeked and famished, nestling together by the potbellied stove while defrosting our limbs from the bitter Romanian winter. In the evening we would hide under the kitchen table. It was way past our bed time, but clearly unnoticed we giggled and enjoyed our purloined moments tucked away under the wooden cloak, peaking at the adults invested in grown-up conversations. These were noble stories, war stories that my grandfather was recalling, full of adventure, danger, friendship, sacrifice, and heroism. My grandma spoke of hard times, being alone with six small children hiding away from the Germans and the Russians. Other stories were of fun times, of different people and places as all the adults' bellies were shaking with laughter and toasting glasses full of homemade cider. I know now that these furtive moments under the farm table have contributed to my understanding of life, helped shape my character, and impressed on me a strong family bond.

My Christian faith developed in that kitchen house. As a little girl, I would watch my grandparents kneel by their beds (they also slept in the kitchen), and pray to God over their open Bible. They told me about Jesus and how wonderful He is. God spoke in that house in my grandpa's voice, in his hard work, in my grandma's gentle humility, her obedience to Christ, and in living her life with seamless faith.

This is the place where I also learned how to cook. If I close my eyes, I can still smell the fresh yeast eagerly frothing in a bowl of warm water, waiting to perform its magical purpose in proudly risen dough. My grandma approached her baking with insight and instinct, supple hands kneading the dough with familiarity which complied under her dexterous fingers. She also bathed me in that kitchen, near the wood-burning stove, in a round galvanized tub, brushing my hair and answering all my innocent (and annoying) questions with patience and wisdom. I learned many things from her, as she was always kind, charitable to others, nonjudgmental, generous, stoical, hardworking, and humble.

I also witnessed commitment and devotion as my grandparents were married for many decades, and still treated each other with respect and love, at times my grandpa kissing his wife's hair on his way out. She would try to stop him in mock annoyance, "Quit that, old man!"

I have to admit that there were plenty of fights in that kitchen house, with slammed doors, family members shouting and punctuating the air with gestures of frustration and anger. But there was also much-needed forgiveness and restoration of broken hearts. Many babies cried in that kitchen, many weddings celebrated, and many funeral wakes attended as time took its toll on the living.

Even now, my go-to image of peace when I'm stressed out is my grandparents' orchard that stretched behind the kitchen house. Flashing bright red, the apple trees festooned the back of the valley with globes of crisp sweetness. With my eyes closed, I still see my childhood sun shuffling in, lazily warming the endless days of summer.

I've lived in many places in my life, experienced different cultures and people, but over two decades later, the kitchen house—the memory room—still remains close to my heart. It may sound silly, but all the lessons I learned, the wisdom bestowed, the joy and love shared, all of it has shaped who I am today.

I wanted my kids to experience a bit of this heaven on earth, so I took them to Romania, introducing them to my roots and theirs. It made me think of Sting's lyrics, "And inside ev'ry turning leaf is the pattern of an older tree, the shape of our future, the shape of all our history." I'm obviously the older tree! My children loved the farm, the kitchen house, the animals, the light that is so alive early in the morning ascending over the breathtaking village, the clotheslines, and the food of course! I didn't allow any electronics, and somehow they survived. My son happily worked around the farm, helping his aunt doing chores, and my girl was in veterinarian heaven tending to all domestic animals possible. It was an extraordinary feeling seeing my own kids immersed in my childhood place, but after two weeks they both asked, "Can we go home now?" *Of course you can. Your memories will be made far away from this place.* So, I took one last walk through the countryside, where rows of poplar trees were standing sentinel to my childhood memories, protecting them, and guarding them from dispersing into new winds.

I hope and pray that my husband and I can give our son and daughter a spectacular childhood, so whatever memories we create with them will be the platform from which they stem forth, and will act as a prism through which they may see themselves as adults. What memories we compile as a family unit will also reflect what kind of legacy we leave behind, hopefully one that God will approve of.

I am not certain that my kids will have a specific "memory room" in mind when looking back on their childhood, but it does seem that we also spend most of our time in the kitchen. We do homework there, talk about our day, eat waddled around that uncomfortably small table, share news, store backpacks, cook together, dance around like crazy to different kinds of music, we parents smooch by the kitchen sink (because for some reason my hubby always gets amorous when I wash dishes!).

Time will do its thing, coaxing us forward, and it feels as though I'm running out of time. I envision myself speed-parenting, cramming in more valuable lessons and yelling them, as my kids step over the childhood threshold and out the adult door—like I used to yell to zip up their coats when my kids were little . . . So, I'm scrambling, *"Umm . . . let's see, think of others before yourselves, it's okay to fail, it's normal to feel pain, the best kind of car is the payed-off kind, laugh out loud as much as possible, be kind, be clean, it's okay to cry in public, always pray for your decisions, shave your legs (to my girl), open the door for the girls (to my son), be good listeners, have compassion, oh my goodness . . . I think I'm forgetting something . . . God cares about what happens to you, what else . . . hmm . . . Oh yeah, and we love you forever and come home often."*

Who needs these kinds of thoughts? . . . Parents. That's who. With my mind still in the future I stress that perhaps I didn't teach them enough, didn't do enough devotionals, that I let them watch PG-13 movies prematurely, that I messed them up! Too late now, they are gone . . .

Of course, by now you must think me entirely crazy, but surely you identify even if just a little, right? Sir Paul McCartney even says it in his song "Ever Present Past": "The time I thought would last, My ever present past . . . It flew by, it flew by in a flash." My husband always says that the days are long but the years fly by . . . Between diapers, birthdays, melted ice cream, frustrated tantrums, and time-outs, growing up happens, and all of a sudden we'll find ourselves fighting back tears on their first day of school, and then nauseated with worry on the first day they drive a car. I ponder at times when I will witness my boy's last sleep in his childhood room, where many times I stroked his tousled toddler curls. I will miss my girl's affection, her soft hands wrapped around my neck as we cuddle on the couch, her sweet smell lingering on my clothes.

I realize that when my son gets married I'll have to hand him over with an instruction manual to make his future wife's life a little easier (he-he), and on my daughter's wedding day there will be a last warning to the groom that if he hurts my girl he'll have to deal with the wrath of the Eastern European mother! (Whatever that means, but I have to sound threatening!)

Don't think that I have these thoughts as I sit alone on the couch. No, I do this to myself as I fold laundry, cook, and then inevitably it dawns on me that for now my babies are still here with me. I'm washing *their* clothes, making *their* favorite after-dinner dessert. Yay! I am still needed and thankfully they are still driving me crazy! These two blessings from God are the most fantastic gifts, and yes one day they will leave, but for now they are here with me and my husband making memories to last a lifetime. As we all tuck around the dinner table, I exhale in unlimited gratitude that these kids are really ours—no other parents are coming to get them, that we really are their parents trusted by God to mold them and shape them according to His will, for our children will definitely turn out to be the most wonderful human beings we have ever met.

"Let the children come to me. Don't stop them! For the Kingdom of God belongs to such as these. . . ." Then he took the children into his arms and placed his hands on their heads and blessed them. (Mark 10:15–16)

Notes

Chapter 1

1. James Dobson, *The New Strong-Willed Child* (Carol Stream, IL: Tyndale Publishers, 2004), 45.

Chapter 8

2. Erwin Raphael McManus, *Artisan Soul: Crafting Your Life into a Work of Art* (New York: HarperCollins, 2014), 37.
3. Ibid.

Chapter 11

4. This quotation is a combination of Dave Ramsey's book *Financial Peace Revisited* (New York: Penguin Group, 2003), 215 and notes taken from a sermon series at LifeChurch entitled "Outlasters: Financially Free Families."

Chapter 14

5. https://en.wikipedia.org/wiki/Selfie.

Chapter 16

6. James Dobson, *The New Strong-Willed Child* (Carol Stream, IL: Tyndale, 2014), 46.
7. A. A. Milne, *The Complete Tales of Winnie-the-Pooh* (New York: Dutton Books, 1926, 1994), 70.

Chapter 18

8. Diane Stark, "Tween Crushes" at http://www.thrivingfamily.com/Family/Stages/Tween%20Ages/2015/tween-crushes.aspx., February/March 2015.
9. This article is from my blog from September 2012. See http://soulpurposemag.com/?p=237.

Acknowledgments

Thank You, Jesus, for molding me in my mother's womb and for being the best loving Father a girl could ever have.

I want to thank my husband, Donny. You are my best friend, my soulmate, my constant supporter. You make me laugh every day and you are a wonderful father to our children. I love you forever. Thank you for inspiring the title of this book.

Thank you to my precious mother who lives in Romania. You are amazing in every way, and taught me to love and to give like no other. Thank you for your sacrifice.

Thank you to the apples of my eye, Harrison and Sofia. You have honored me in being your mother. Thank you for allowing me to share your lives with the world. Having you is like Christmas morning every day: the sweetest gifts I get to love on forever. I am in awe that you are ours and I thank God for giving you to us.

The most special thanks to the best of friends, and best of editors, Amanda Sauer. You humble me in every way, with your generosity, kindness, grace, talent, and ability. If it wasn't for you, this book would still sit lifeless on my desk. Thank you for believing in me, supporting me, and pushing me to plough through my huge self-doubt.

Thank you to Ark House Publishing. Thank you, Nicole and Matt Danswan, for taking a chance on me. Nicole, you have my deepest gratitude for being the first one to make me a published author at *Christian Woman* magazine. You have changed my life.

Thank you to Pam Walrond for giving me my first job as a payed writer.

Thank you to Rene and Stan Fields, our greatest of friends, and role models in parenting. You are family and I love you dearly.

Thank you to Kay Darnel, my precious gem of a friend, who never doubted my ability as a writer. Your vision seeing me at a book signing is coming true! Love you.

Thank you to Lori and Don Dixon for praying with me when I am a complete mess. Lori, you are the best sister-in-law, and I treasure you as a sister, friend, and writer.

Very special thanks to my stepdaughter, Angela, who has first introduced me to parenting many moons ago. You are easy to love.

Thank you to my partner in crime, my cousin Oana. Growing up with you in our grandparents' house, will always be part of my childhood memories.

Thank you to my other two cousins, Daniela and Diana. Together, we will always be the four girls Bica and Bicu got to spoil.

I wish Virginia and Gheorghe were here so I could thank them for being my grandparents. They were the greatest role models of a happy marriage, patience, wisdom, and godliness. They had six children, including my mother, and I am honored to have been born in our family. I miss them forever.

To my dearest aunts, Maia and Doina, you are my other two moms. I miss you every day from far away. You have enriched my childhood with laughter and love.

My uncles, Mihai, Vasile, Dan, Petrica, and Telucu have passed, but I want to remember them for stepping in and role-modeling father figures in my life. They hugged me, taught me how to ride a bike, made me midnight snacks, encouraged me to stay brave, and also slipped money in my pocket!

Thank you to Pastor Craig Groeschel for your guidance .You and your wife inspire me in bringing up six godly children.

Thank you to Pastor Aaron and Crystal for loving on my children before you had your own. You two are spectacular beings!

Thank you to Stacy Edwards, Michelle Coomer, Nancy Juma, Cari Garrett, Katrina Henderson, Barby Harmon, Gretchen DeVries, and Adrienne McDonald for giving me such encouragement.

Thank you Nick and Ashley Thompson for role modeling enduring faith and strength. You are inspiring!

Thank you, Bernie Herms and Natalie Grant, for taking the time to read my book and giving it a great review. It means so much to me.

I have to thank Jane Austen, whose quote —"I can always live by my pen"—is giving me the courage to put ink to paper.

Thank you to all the parents out there who are willing to accept my transparency in this book. I hope you laugh, cry, and identify, for we are in this together!

CPSIA information can be obtained at www.ICGtesting.com
Printed in the USA
LVOW10s0534230916

505856LV00001B/1/P

9 780994 596833